Absolute Crime

CW00855518

Getting Away W

15 Chilling Cold Cases That Will Make You Think Twice About Going Outside

ABSO(UTE CR**I**ME

By William Webb

Absolute Crime Books

www.absolutecrime.com

Cover Image © bradcalkins - Fotolia.com

Table of Contents

About Us

Absolute Crime publishes only the best true crime literature. Our focus is on the crimes that you've probably never heard of, but you are fascinated to read more about. With each engaging and gripping story, we try to let readers relive moments in history that some people have tried to forget.

Remember, our books are not meant for the faint at heart. We don't hold back — if a crime is bloody, we let the words splatter across the page so you can experience the crime in the most horrifying way!

If you enjoy this book, please visit our homepage to see other books we offer; if you have any feedback, we'd love to hear from you!

Introduction

Despite a decline in the number of murders in the United States since the 1960s, thousands go unsolved each year. As of 2013, the solve rate was at an all time low at only 65 percent of the total committed. The following 15 murders were committed between 1958 and 2014. The oldest of the set involves the bizarre murder of Pearl Eaton, one of the famous Ziegfeld Follies Girls of the 1920s. From the beginning, the crime had no leads or suspects and remains among the coldest of the 15 unsolved crimes. The most recent – the murder of four members of the McStay family found buried in the California desert in November 2013 – is under active investigation.

1991 Austin Yogurt Shop Murders

At about 11 P.M. on the night of December 6, 1991, four teenage girls were closing a yogurt shop in north Austin, Texas. Shortly before midnight, the Austin Fire Department responded to a fire at the same location. Fire and police officials thinking they were responding to a structural fire were horrified to discover the bodies of the four teens among the rubble. The first police officer to enter the building described the scene as wholesale carnage. Twenty-three years later, no one is in prison for the crime.

Jennifer Harbison and Eliza Thomas, both age 17, worked in the *I Can't Believe it is Yogurt!* shop located in a strip mall at 2949 West Anderson Lane in Austin, Texas. Jennifer's sister Sarah Harbison, age 15, and a 13-year-old friend Amy Ayers, joined the two girls at the shop on the night of December 6, 1991, to help with closing. All four girls were later described by family, friends, and school officials as wholesome, full of life, and popular with their classmates.

Sometime after closing, one or more assailants shot three of the teens in the back of the head once and the fourth girl twice. Both .22 and .380 caliber weapons were used. The fourth girl was also strangled and one, perhaps two, of the teens was sexually assaulted. All four girls were stripped of their clothes and bound and gagged with them. Three of the bodies were piled on top of one another in the back room of the shop. The youngest teen tried to escape and was killed near the front door and the empty cash drawer was found next to her body. The front door still had the key in the lock – a detail that required first responders to break down the door.

To eliminate any witnesses and cover up the crime – which may have started out as a robbery – the assailants piled Styrofoam cups on the bodies, poured lighter fluid on them, and set the store on fire. A patrolling police officer notified the Fire Department at 11:47 P.M. When the wristwatch was later removed from Jennifer Harbison's arm, the time read 11:48.

The coroner determined that all four girls were dead before the fire was started and each had extensive burns. Even though they were all shot in the back of the head execution style, they were all four found lying face up on the yogurt shop's floor.

Eyewitnesses and customers from the night of the crime were able to offer clues to the last few hours in the yogurt shop. Among them was a former police officer and security company owner who noticed a tall, thin, young man in a green camouflage jacket. Acting oddly, the man went to the back of the store to use the restroom but never returned. Suspicious, the security company owner later told police he feared the man had waited until the store was closed and the front door locked and then let in an accomplice through the back door. The man in the green jacket was never identified.

Just before 11 P.M., a married couple noticed two men sitting in one of the yogurt shop's booths. In their account, the couple stated the men were acting strangely and made them uncomfortable, much like the account of the man in the green jacket. When the couple left the shop, the two men were still there watching the girls as they filled empty napkin containers and turned empty chairs upside down on the tables. Even though the fire destroyed most of the shop's interior, crime scene photos clearly reveal the booth described by the couple. The napkin container was still empty and there were no chairs placed on the table of that one booth. The two men could not be located.

Over the years, there was a long list of suspects. For unclear reasons, more than 50 people, mostly teens, confessed to the crime and hundreds more were interviewed. Within the first 2 weeks, there were 25 possible leads. These included a teenaged girl and her boyfriend who confessed, but ultimately knew no accurate details of the crime; a group of suspected drug dealers found through a 911 tip, but with airtight alibis; and two men previously suspected of murdering two Austin convenience store clerks. Each lead was investigated, but all were dead ends.

At times, the Austin police were convinced that an arrest was imminent, at other times, there were no viable leads, and the case was cold. The Federal Bureau of Investigation's Behavioral Science Unit at Quantico, Virginia, generated a profile of the killers – white males, age 17 to 28; emotionally immature and easily angered – and 20 large billboards donated by local businesses were erected all over the city. The billboards displayed photographs of each girl and offered a reward, which over time rose from $25,000 to $100,000. Although the billboards generated more than 2,000 tips, the reward went unclaimed. An artist's sketch of a man frequently seen parked in a car outside the yogurt shop also was distributed to the public, but provided no new leads. The crime also received national attention when it was the subject of episodes of *48 Hours* (March 1992) and *America's Most Wanted* (August 1992).

In the Spring of 1993, the Austin police added six new officers to the original 12-man task force investigating the murders. With no new leads, the additional staff cleared a backlog of several thousand tips before the task force disbanded. Two homicide detectives stayed on to monitor the investigation and an FBI agent, an Austin arson investigator, and an agent from the Department of Alcohol, Tobacco, and Firearms continued on full time.

By December 1993, the door to the yogurt shopped had been bricked over and the windows darkened and reinforced. The space was eventually converted for other retail purposes and is no longer recognizable as the yogurt shop. A bronze marker naming all four of the victims was placed in a grassy area of the strip mall parking lot.

Over 2,500 people attended the joint memorial service for the four girls. Three of the teens – Jennifer, Sarah, and Amy – were buried next to each other and a memorial bench placed at the gravesite.

In late 1992, three Mexican nationals charged in the kidnapping and rape of a woman outside an Austin nightclub were questioned in the yogurt shop murders and one even confessed to the crime. Two of the men later recanted their accounts saying they were forced to make false statements and all three men were eventually removed from the suspect list and never charged in the crime.

Kenneth Allen McDuff, who was executed by the state of Texas in 1998 for a series of brutal crimes between 1965 and 1992, was questioned repeatedly about the yogurt shop killings, but denied any involvement. An unnamed source told an Austin television station that McDuff confessed to the yogurt shop murders on the day he was executed, but investigators said key details of the crime were incorrect and they did not believe the confession. Given his long violent history, including the kidnapping and murder of three teens in Fort Worth, McDuff likely had the answers to numerous unsolved crimes, but took that information to his death.

The last of the viable suspects were four men who were arrested in 1999. At the time of the crime, all four were teens and two were juveniles. Michael James Scott (25), Forrest Welborn (23), and Maurice Earl Pierce (24) were arrested in Texas; Robert Burns Springsteen (24) was arrested and extradited from West Virginia. Information leading to the arrests originated with a 1997 interview with Pierce, who was caught with a .22-caliber pistol in a shopping mall a few days after the killings. Pierce told the police that it was the weapon used in the yogurt shop murders, but that Welborn had the gun at the time. After several interviews, police determined that both were lying and no charges were filed.

The interrogation of Pierce and Welborn eventually led to the questioning of Springsteen and Scott, both of whom confessed to the crime but also implicated Pierce and Welborn. All four were arrested in October (1999) and charged with capital murder. After 8 years without any solid suspects, the residents of Austin thought the police had finally caught the killers. At trial, the prosecuting attorney insisted that Springsteen entered the store earlier in the evening and fixed the rear door lock so that his accomplices could enter later for a robbery. When the men discovered four teens at closing instead of two, they murdered the four girls and tried to cover up the crime by burning down the building.

Between 1999 and 2009, cases against each of the four men were repeatedly in and out of court. Both Welborn and Pierce were juveniles at the time of the crime and there was a court battle over whether to try them as adults. While that was taking place, Grand Juries twice refused to indict Welborn, who was accused of being a lookout and the getaway driver. Pierce insisted on his innocence admitting only to being with the other three the night *after* the crime. Based on a lack of evidence, all charges against Welborn were eventually dropped in June 2000.

Because he was a juvenile at the time of the murders, Pierce faced life in prison. Having only a minor arrest record prior to the murders and with no hard evidence to hold him, all charges were dropped in January 2003. Pierce remained haunted by the experience. Even though he had been exonerated, the police continued to consider him a prime suspect and family members later commented that Pierce feared he would eventually be rearrested for the crime. On the night of December 23, 2010, Pierce reportedly ran a stop sign and when Austin police officers attempted to stop him, he pulled the car to the side of the road and fled on foot. An altercation subsequently occurred and Pierce reportedly grabbed a knife from one of the officer's belts and stabbed him in the throat. The officer survived, but managed to fire a single shot that fatally killed Pierce.

The District Attorney's office asked for the death penalty for Springsteen and Scott arguing that the two men knew details of the crime that only the killers would know. Defense attorneys argued that the police coerced Springsteen and Scott into their confessions and a photograph surfaced of an Austin police detective holding a gun to Scott's head in an interrogation room. Although the District Attorney vigorously denied the charge, the detective was eventually fired.

In 2001, Springsteen was convicted of capital murder and given the death penalty. In 2005, his sentence was commuted to life in prison after the Supreme Court ruled that executing juvenile killers was unconstitutional. In 2008, Springsteen was granted a new trial by the Texas Court of Criminal Appeals on the basis that he had been unfairly convicted. Using the Sixth Amendment of the U.S. Constitution as a basis for the argument, Springfield's attorney argued that he had been convicted using a written statement from his co-defendant Scott. The Texas court ruled that Springsteen had been denied the constitutional right to confront his accuser.

Scott was sentenced to life in prison in 2002 during a separate trial. As with Springsteen's case, Scott's attorney argued that Springsteen's confession helped to convict Scott and Scott's confession helped to convict Springsteen, but neither was afforded their Constitutional right to confront the other. In June 2009, both convictions were overturned on this technicality and Scott and Springsteen were released on bond. Prosecutors vowed to retry both.

Complicating a potential retrial of the remaining two suspects, FBI ballistics tests showed that the handgun owned by Pierce was not the murder weapon. The second weapon – a .380 caliber semi-automatic pistol believed to have been owned by Springsteen – was never found. Most significantly, DNA samples taken from the murder scene were tested in 2008 and found to be from two, possibly three, unknown males. None matched any of the four suspects. Defense attorneys argued that the DNA belonged to the real killers and proved that the confessions had been coerced. Prosecuting attorneys argued the DNA samples were either contaminated and/or that the four original suspects were aided by additional accomplices.

In February 2013, Defense Attorneys for Scott and Springsteen requested DNA testing of alternative suspects to look for matches to the unidentified male samples found at the crime scene. The testing would include serial killer Kenneth McDuff, who was executed in 1998. Additional DNA tests for the alternative suspects have not yet been conducted.

Based on the ballistics tests and the lack of a DNA match to either Springsteen or Scott, the District Attorney dismissed all charges against the two men on October 28, 2009. Despite a complete lack of evidence from the crime scene, as of 2014, Scott and Springsteen continue to be prime suspects in the yogurt shop murders. Although their convictions have been overturned, the Court did not issue a judicial declaration of innocence. As a result, they are not eligible for restitution for the years they were wrongfully incarcerated. Springsteen is actively pursuing his innocence and, ultimately, restitution in the Texas Civil Court system.

Abner Zwillman

February 26, 1959: He was found hanged with plastic rope from a water pipe in the basement of his mansion in West Orange, New Jersey. A three-page obituary in the *New York Daily News* called it suicide, but there were telltale bruises on his wrists and ankles showing he had been bound. While his death technically remains unsolved, Abner *Longie* Zwillman, age 55, was probably silenced.

February 27, 1959: Barely 24 hours after his body was found, 350 souls were crowded into the Apter Funeral Home; 1,500 others stood outside. Among the crowd were Hollywood producers, politicians, businessmen, and the simply curious. New Jersey's Third Ward had lost its most notorious and legendary resident.

Abner Zwillman was one of seven children born to impoverished Russian Jewish immigrants. He was born in Newark, New Jersey, on July 27, 1904, while the family lived on Charlton Street, just west of Newark's Prince Street shopping area. Charlton Street was also just four blocks from the notorious Broome Street and its many saloons. Because of his tall thin frame, the oldest son of the Zwillman's was nicknamed *Longie*, a name that he carried his entire life.

As a child, Abner ran errands for pocket change; most of his clients were bookies and pimps. When his father died in 1918, Abner, age 14, left the Charlton Street School, where he had just completed the eighth grade. His older sister Bessie was trying to support the family, but the pay of a stenographer in an insurance office was not enough, so Abner went to work in a Prince Street café. Because Abner and Bessie's combined salaries were still not enough, Abner rented a horse and wagon and began selling produce on the streets of New Jersey's Third Ward. As a low-income area, most of the residents of the Ward could not afford Abner's fruits and vegetables, so he moved his business to the more affluent Clinton Hill neighborhood. Soon realizing that the housewives in Clinton Hill were more interested in lottery numbers than produce, Abner changed his business model and set up his own numbers bank that included an organized network of drug stores, saloons, and other small shops. The shops collected bets for Abner in exchange for a $30 per week salary. Dedicated to his family and not wanting them to be hungry ever again, Abner used his wiles to create considerable wealth and before he was 20 years old, he controlled the numbers business in almost all of Newark.

Living in, and working primarily from, the Jewish neighborhoods around Newark's Prince Street, Zwillman and his *Happy Ramblers* gang also protected local businesses and families from seemingly endless anti-Semitic harassment and assault. Threats of trouble were met with *Ruff der Langer* – the Yiddish expression for *Call the Tall One*, and those calls were always quickly answered.

Zwillman also funded Newark's soup kitchens during the Depression years, paid for the shipment of weapons to Israel during their fight for independence, ensured that Jewish families had food baskets during holidays, and had trucks distribute food and toys to Christian families at Christmas.

For these many kindnesses, and despite his known criminal associations, Zwillman earned the life-long gratitude and respect of those he helped.

The Volstead Act was enacted in 1920 as the means to enforce the Eighteenth Amendment of the Constitution. The Amendment and Act prohibited the manufacture and sale of alcoholic beverages anywhere in the United States. Undaunted by the legislation and recognizing the opportunity for a lucrative business, Abner Zwillman and his partners – known as the Big Seven Group – became one of the most dominant bootlegging operations on the east coast. Members of the group included Zwillman and Enoch *Nucky* Johnson (both from New Jersey), Moe Dalitz (from Cleveland), Waxey Gordon and Harry *Nig* Rose (from Philadelphia), and Danny Walsh (from Providence, Rhode Island). By the late 1920s, the group was also supported by Italian Charles *Lucky* Luciano and Meyer Lansky, a Russian operating out of Florida.

Using refurbished World War I armored trucks, the powerful organization smuggled thousands of cases of illegal liquor into the United States from Canada and distributed it from Zwillman's warehouses in the Third Ward. The group had a lot of help from their political and law enforcement allies as well. Police often either looked the other way, or more overtly provided protection along the truck routes or at the warehouses to make sure the goods were not hijacked. By the time Prohibition ended in 1933, Zwillman's group controlled more than 40 percent of the illegal alcohol trade in the United States – reportedly more than Al Capone.

Between the end of Prohibition and the time he died, Zwillman used his money, good looks, and charm to diversify. His operations included both illegal activities – prostitution, gambling, racketeering – and legal operations. Zwillman owned legitimate restaurants, hotels, and nightclubs that generated millions of dollars each year and he used his power and influence to befriend, or control, entertainers, politicians, and labor unions. Zwillman had a brief affair with the movie star Jean Harlow in the early 1930s and was briefly suspected in the unusual death of her husband Paul Bern. Bern's death was later ruled suicide, although some thought that Harlow herself had murdered him. Zwillman also reportedly loaned Harry Cohn the money to establish Columbia Pictures and paid him $500,000 to cast Harlow in his films.

Through these years, Zwillman maintained his roots to New Jersey's Third Ward and ran his operations from the Riviera Hotel.

While Zwillman's operations were mostly legitimate, by the early 1950s his ties to the underworld remained strong and often laced with conflict. In 1957, he crossed Vito Genovese, the powerful mob boss from New York, when he did not support Genovese's efforts to oust rival Frank Costello, as head of the powerful Luciano family. Instead, Zwillman supported Albert Anastasia, who Genovese promptly had killed. With several of his allies dead and two others – Meyer Lansky and Moe Dalitz – focusing on their operations in Cuba and Las Vegas, Zwillman, the once undisputed New Jersey crime boss, was vulnerable to Genovese. Now aging and alone, Genovese and others started eyeing Zwillman's territory. To make matters worse, Zwillman was being harassed by the Internal Revenue Service for tax evasion, and, in early 1959, was issued a subpoena to testify before Senator John McClellan's Committee investigating organized crime's infiltration of U.S. labor unions. As reported in the media, committee member John F. Kennedy (not yet the President) and Kennedy's brother Robert, who was then White House Chief General Council, were looking forward to questioning him before the public. They never got the chance.

The investigation into Abner Zwillman's death was inconclusive, but reports of suicide were probably a cover for the true method of death. Ligature marks on his wrists and ankles were part of the inconsistency and it appeared to most that his death was more like an ordered hit. Zwillman admitted that he did not want to go to jail for tax evasion. He also did not want to testify before the Senate and former allies were afraid he would become an informer to avoid prison.

Allies and enemies alike insisted they played no part in Zwillman's death, but Meyer Lansky told a biographer some years later that the hit was ordered by Genovese, even though he was behind bars at the time on narcotics charges. Lucky Luciano laid the blame on Carlo Gambino for a past indiscretion, but almost everyone agreed that Zwillman would not have been executed without the approval of Lansky and a vote by the senior crime bosses.

Although accounts vary and the origin of the order has never been confirmed, both law enforcement and the east coast underworld believe that Zwillman was executed. As the story goes, he was told in advance that he had to die. When Zwillman resisted, he was plied with expensive brandy to ease the pain, tied at the hands and ankles, and hung from the water pipes in his luxury mansion. It was a gesture of respect.

Abner *Longie* Zwillman's funeral included seven chauffer-driven limousines, 27 private cars, and almost 2,000 attendees. As reported in the media – it was the biggest event of its kind in the history of New Jersey's Third Ward.

Arlis Perry

Memorial Church is situated at the west entrance to Stanford University in Palo Alto, California. Known as MemChu by students and faculty, the 112-year-old non-denominational church is small, but beautifully detailed with stained glass windows, intricate ceiling tiles, and murals. Throughout its long history, the church has been the setting for countless religious ceremonies, two damaging earthquakes (1906 and 1989), and one of the most famous, frustrating, and sensational crimes ever investigated by the Santa Clara County Sheriff's Department. Forty years after Arlis Kay Dykema Perry from Bismark, North Dakota, was murdered near the church's ornate altar, the crime remains unsolved.

At about 11:30 on the night of October 12, 1974, newlyweds Bruce and Arlis Perry walked across the Stanford University grounds to drop some letters in the campus mailbox. They were both 19 years old.

Along the way, the couple argued about a leaking tire on their car and who should have it fixed. Somewhat annoyed with each other, Arlis decided to stop at Memorial Church and let her husband continue to their apartment in Quillen Hall alone. Bruce, a Stanford pre-med sophomore, later told police that he thought twice about letting her go without him, but that it was not unusual for them to worship at the small church at odd hours. The two separated about a half-mile from their apartment: the time was 11:40 P.M.

Approximately 10 minutes later, Arlis entered the church, walked to the front left row, and knelt to pray. Nearing midnight – the time when the church doors were locked for the day – there were only two others in the church; both remembered seeing the young woman in the brown jacket and blue jeans and both left the church at midnight recalling that Arlis was still in prayer.

Shortly after Arlis was left alone in the church, a passerby noticed someone entering. The eyewitness described the person as a young man, perhaps 23-25 years old wearing a blue short-sleeved shirt and no wristwatch. The man was about 5-foot 10 inches tall, had a medium build, and his hair was sandy-colored and parted on the left.

At 12:10 A.M. campus security guard Steve Crawford entered the church to make sure it was empty and called out that the church was closing for the night. Crawford neither heard nor saw anyone, but he did not walk past the front foyer. Certain that the church was empty, the security guard exited through the front doors and locked them for the night. Crawford later told authorities that he returned to the church around 2 A.M. to make sure all the doors were locked, but saw and heard nothing.

By around midnight, Bruce Perry had become increasingly concerned that his wife was not home, so he left their apartment and walked in the direction of the church to find her. When he found the doors to the church locked, Bruce wandered though the campus in search of her, but she was nowhere to be found. Hoping they had taken different routes and that she was already safely at home, Bruce returned to the apartment. It was empty.

Police records show that Bruce Perry made a call to campus security to report his wife missing at 3 A.M. He suggested that perhaps Arlis had fallen asleep in one of the pews and was locked inside the church. A follow-up visit by campus security indicated that nothing unusual was seen or heard and supported Crawford's 2 A.M. report that all of the doors were locked.

When Crawford returned to the church at 5:30 A.M., he found the door at the right side of the church had been forced open. – not from the outside, but from the inside – as if someone had been locked in. Initially, Crawford saw nothing amiss, but within minutes of searching in and around the pews, he discovered the body of Arlis Perry carefully arranged on the floor of the left (east) transept.

Assuming the validity of the security police reports that all the doors were locked at 12:10 A.M., 2 A.M., and 3AM, and based on the time of death set by the Medical Examiner – approximately midnight – the killer of Arlis Perry was still inside the church when Bruce checked the front door at 12:15 and the security checks were made. Given these assumptions, the killer would not have forced his way out of the right church door until sometime between 3 A.M. and 5:30 A.M. when the body was found. Even with the details of the crime and the amount of time it might have taken the assailant to prepare the body, it is unlikely that the killer would have remained at the crime scene for more than 3 hours. There is, however, no evidence to confirm otherwise.

Found near where she was last seen praying, Arlis Perry was lying on her back beneath the last pew of the east transept. The young woman had been severely beaten and strangled and her body was naked from the waist down with her legs spread apart; her head was towards the main altar. The blue jeans she had been wearing were placed across her legs in the shape of the letter V. When seen against her spread legs, the jeans created a ritualistic pattern similar to a diamond. Her blouse and brown jacket had been ripped open and a 24-inch-long altar candle was placed between her breasts. A similar altar candle was forced into her vagina with such force that it had snapped in two; forensics later determined that it carried a clear palm print. Arlis had not been raped, but semen stains were found on a nearby kneeling cushion.

Although grotesque in method and presentation, Arlis Perry's actual cause of death was an ice pick wound to the head. The 5 ½-inch weapon had been viciously thrust into her skull behind the left ear and its metal portion discovered during the autopsy; the presence/absence of the weapon's handle at the scene of the crime is unclear. Given that an ice pick is not the type of item typically found in a church, authorities concluded that the murder was premeditated. As later described by church officials and crime scene investigators, Arlis Perry's murder was truly a sight from Hell.

Two personal items were removed from the crime scene, either as souvenirs or as proof of the murder. One was Arlis' eyeglasses, but the nature of the second has never been released. Two weeks after her burial in Bismark, the temporary cross marking her grave was stolen.

Arlis and Bruce Perry had only recently moved to the Palo Alto area from Bismark, North Dakota. As a sophomore, Bruce had been at Stanford for about a year; Arlis joined him less than 6 weeks before she was killed. As new arrivals, they had only a few friends and acquaintances in California.

The only unusual circumstance associated with the couple was the presence of a second Bruce Duncan Perry already listed by the telephone company at Stanford when Arlis and Bruce were setting up their account. When authorities checked that odd fact during the investigation, they found no trace of him.

Four weeks after joining her husband at Stanford, Arlis was hired as a receptionist at a Palo Alto law firm. Around noon on the day before her murder, Arlis was visited at her new workplace by a man that coworkers initially thought was her husband Bruce. The man was described as having a medium build, about 5-foot 10 inches tall, and in his 20s. He wore jeans and a plaid shirt and had curly, blondish hair. The conversation between Arlis and her visitor lasted about 15 minutes and appeared intense to those who witnessed it. At its conclusion, Arlis returned to her desk, saying nothing to anyone in the firm about the man. Those who assumed the man was her husband were later surprised to learn that it was not Bruce. Bruce told police he had never visited Arlis at work and that he knew of no one fitting the description of the man seen there. The description of the workplace visitor was a match to the man who entered the church just before Arlis was killed.

Based on the unusual posing of Arlis' body by a church altar, there have been persistent theories that the crime showed symbolic characteristics of the occult. Authorities have been outwardly lukewarm to this theory, but it is also possible that they purposefully chose not to attribute occult overtones to the crime. Either way, possible links to satanic cults continue to this day.

During the 18-month period between February 1973 and Arlis' murder in October 1974, there were four baffling murders involving Stanford University students. Including Arlis, there were three women – all strangled, but none raped – and one man who was stabbed 15 times. There were no signs of struggle with any of the victims – as if they were suddenly surprised – and robbery was not a motive. In one case, the mayor of San Francisco reportedly theorized that the crime was committed by the Death Angels, a cult of four African Americans who killed 14 people and wounded eight, mostly Caucasian, between 1973 and 1974. The Death Angel cult members were arrested and convicted in 1975 and sentenced to life in prison; the four Stanford murders remain unsolved.

Based on the setting of the crime and the ritualistic posing of the body, police believed the crime was the work of a sexual psychopath. Other theories have been developed over the last four decades, but the psychopath premise persists. FBI profilers described the killer as between 17 and 22 years old, probably a loner, and someone that would be likely to take a souvenir from the crime scene.

The initial suspect was Arlis' husband Bruce. When Santa Clara County Sheriff's deputies arrived at their apartment to notify him of her death, they were shocked to see Bruce covered in blood. After a bit of explanation (a nosebleed), a blood test (Bruce's type not Arlis'), and a polygraph to establish the truthfulness of his alibi, it was determined that Bruce was no longer a suspect. His palm print did not match the one found on the altar candle, and later DNA testing proved his profile was not a match.

Because he found the body, the second suspect was campus security officer Steve Crawford. Crawford was cleared when his alibi was confirmed and there was no match to the palm print. DNA testing later confirmed his innocence.

Eyewitnesses provided descriptions of seven individuals who visited the Stanford Church during the late night hours of the murder. Over the course of the investigation, six were identified and cleared of the crime. The seventh individual and third suspect – referred to as the sexual psychopathic – was the sandy-haired man seen entering the church just before Arlis was killed and, likely, the same man that had visited her workplace the day before. That suspect was never identified or located. For unknown reasons, the police did not circulate a sketch of this suspect in either California or North Dakota.

David Berkowitz, the infamous Son of Sam cult killer implied that he knew Arlis' killer, but never provided concrete information. Detectives from Santa Clara interviewed Berkowitz at Attica State Prison in New York, but felt he was being less than truthful. The only hint of truth in the Berkowitz connection was a hand-scrawled note in a book he once owned about witchcraft. The book contained an extensive section on the Process Church of the Final Judgment, a nationwide cult dedicated to violence and chaos in order to create a world of satanic glory. Infamous members of this cult included not only Berkowitz, but also Charles Manson, and William Mentzer (the convicted killer of Hollywood producer Roy Radin).

In the margin of the book, Berkowitz wrote *Arlis Perry hunted, stalked and slain, followed to California, Stanford University*. This was perhaps a reference to her murder for having visited a Bismark-area satanic cult with a friend, in hopes of converting them to Christianity. While friends and family in Bismark definitely recalled Arlis' enthusiastic attempts to convert others, none knew specifics about the cult visit or who the second woman might be.

Investigative journalist and author of *The Ultimate Evil* Maury Terry, and Bismark college professor Jon Martinson, believe the North Dakota satanic cult that Arlis visited – and perhaps saw or heard something she should not have – was associated with the Process Church of the Final Judgment and is directly responsible for her death. They also believe that the mysterious sandy-haired man followed her from Bismark to Stanford as their messenger of death.

Hundreds of individuals have been interviewed since the Perry crime was committed and dozens either eliminated by the palm print, verifiable alibis, DNA testing, or polygraph tests. The cleared suspects included well-known killer Ted Bundy, who mentioned a murder in California during one of his confessions. Seattle, Washington, police provided evidence that Bundy was either in Seattle or in custody in Utah at the time of Arlis' murder.

DNA samples and the palm print have been entered into various federal and state databases, but there have been no matches to the samples from the Perry crime scene.

In 2004, Santa Clara County deputies collected cigarette butts from an individual that refused to donate a DNA sample, but the analysis was inconclusive.

As of March 2014, there are no clear suspects. The case remains open but inactive.

Betsy Aardsma

In a dark aisle of Pennsylvania State University's Pattee Library, a pretty, young graduate student lay dying. No one saw the crime committed, and the red jumper dress she wore masked the blood from the stab wound to her heart. First responders believed the 22-year-old coed had fainted or suffered a seizure, and library staff thought little of the unidentified man who walked briskly from the area remarking that a woman in the central stacks (bookshelves) needed help. The date was November 28, 1969. Forty-five years later, the brutal crime remains unsolved.

Betsy Ruth Aardsma spent Thanksgiving Day 1969 with her fiancé David Wright, a medical student at Pennsylvania State College of Medicine in Hershey, Pennsylvania. The following day, Aardsma returned to classes at her campus – Penn State in College Park – to work on a research paper for her English 501 class.

According to police reports and eyewitness accounts, Aardsma and her roommate left their dormitory – Frances Atherton Hall – and took the 9-minute walk to Pattee Library, arriving just before 4P.M. The two parted at the library, promising to meet later for dinner. Aardsma's first stop was a short visit with Harrison Meserole, one of her English professors, whose office was in the library's basement. From there, she dropped her coat at a desk on the third level, and then made a brief stop at the card catalog on the main floor. Around 4:30 P.M., Aardsma descended the narrow steps to a windowless, dimly lit area of the library known as the Level 2 core stacks. Library staff recalled seeing Aardsma searching through books located between Rows 50 and 51.

Shortly thereafter, Penn State student Marilee Erdely, who was studying at a nearby desk, heard what sounded like books falling to the floor. This was almost immediately followed by a man (or perhaps two men, depending on the account) emerging from the bookshelves where Aardsma had been seen browsing. The man led Erdely to Rows 50-51 stating that a girl needed help and that he would go for assistance. The man never returned and a person fitting his description was seen running from the library. Erdely found the motionless Aardsma on the floor surrounded by books, but seeing no blood, thought she had fainted. Erdely's shouts for help went largely unanswered for several minutes. When campus Health Center emergency personnel arrived shortly after 5 P.M., one of the EMTs believed he felt a pulse and Aardsma was quickly taken to the Ritenour Health Center for care. At the Health Center, Aardsma was examined by Dr. Elmer Reed and pronounced dead at 5:20 P.M., although he had not yet identified the cause of death.

Because Penn State's police force consisted primarily of students, serious crimes that took place on campus were investigated by the Pennsylvania State Police, who Dr. Reed notified at approximately 6 P.M. When State Police Trooper Mike Simmers arrived, Dr. Reed removed Aardsma's red dress, discovered a stab wound, and subsequently transferred her body to Centre Community Hospital in Bellefonte for autopsy. Simmers took the clothing into evidence and, along with Dr. Reed, preliminarily determined the cause of death to be homicide.

The autopsy at Centre Community Hospital was conducted by pathologist Thomas Magnani. In his report, Dr. Magnani described a single raindrop-shaped puncture wound to the center of Aardsma's chest, which severed the pulmonary artery, punctured the heart, and nicked the tissue behind it. Although the murder weapon was never found, Dr. Magnani described it as a single-edged, four-inch blade similar to a sturdy hunting knife. The pathologist further stated that bruising around the puncture and penetration of the breastbone indicated that the injury would have required significant strength and that the wound caused rapid and profuse internal bleeding. Betsy Ruth Aardsma displayed no defensive wounds or signs of a struggle and likely knew her killer; she would have survived less than 5 minutes after the attack.

Within a few days, the State Police established a command center on campus and had approximately 20 Troopers investigating the murder. The police interviewed hundreds of College Park students and faculty members, some of whom were in the library at the time of the crime. The leads were of little help. A man described as early 20s, with blond hair and wearing khaki pants, a plaid shirt, and tennis shoes was seen running from the library immediately after the crime, but was never identified and composite sketches were too generic to be useful. The university offered a $25,000 reward, but no one came forward.

Over the 45 years since the murder of Betsy Aardsma occurred, the official State Police files have grown to more than 2,000 pages; however, because the case is still open and active, the files are sealed to the public. Rumors persist that the State Police had a strong suspect from the beginning of the investigation, but insufficient evidence for an arrest. In addition, the Penn State newspaper *The Daily Collegian*, has removed numerous articles related to the case from their public archives.

Because of the angle of the wound and the force required to inflict the single lethal injury, the State Police and all others that have investigated this crime believe the perpetrator was male.

At the time of the murder, there were numerous students in the library on the roster for English Class 501. Professor Meserole and Professor Nicholas Joukovsky, who taught the class together, extended their office hours the day Aardsma was killed to give students the opportunity to discuss their research. According to an interview with Joukovsky in 2008, the types of material needed for English 501 research was located in the Level 2 core stacks. There were at least 40 students signed-up for the class and the killer's name may be among them.

Robert Durgy was an assistant professor of English who taught at the University of Michigan, Ann Arbor, where a rash of murders occurred between 1967 and 1969 and where Betsy Aardsma attended undergraduate school. Durgy transferred to Penn State College Park, at exactly the same time Aardsma began her classes in September 1969. Interviews with the staff at Penn State indicated that Durgy appeared under unusual stress and abruptly left Penn State around Thanksgiving. Approximately 2 weeks later, Durgy died in an unexplained car crash. Although the circumstances surrounding Durgy were suspicious for both the serial Michigan murders of the late 1960s (some unsolved) and Aardsma's death, several sources verified that he was in Michigan at the time of her death.

Given the precision of the solitary wound, the murder investigation initially focused squarely on Aardsma's medical student fiancé, David Wright. Wright's alibi was that he was studying gross anatomy with fellow students. The Pennsylvania State Police repeatedly questioned Wright, but several classmates supported his alibi and he eventually was eliminated from the list of potential suspects.

A second boyfriend – Richard (Rick) Haefner – was a Geology doctoral student at Penn State, College Park. Although officially not considered a suspect, he was the subject of interest in the Aardsma murder. The two dated briefly in the fall of 1969, breaking up just before Thanksgiving. Haefner was known to wear plaid shirts and khaki slacks almost exclusively and displayed odd behavior both before and after Aardsma's death. Between the 1970s and late 1990s, Haefner was involved in, or arrested for, violence against women, aggravated assault, sexual molestation, pedophilia, and displayed a volatile temper. A neighbor from Lancaster, Pennsylvania, described him as brilliant, but a terror. On the night of Aardsma's murder, Haefner appeared at the home of a Penn State professor claiming he had read about Aardsma's murder in the newspaper, but this conversation occurred before her name, or the specifics of the crime were published.

In the mid 1970s, Haefner also was overheard confessing to *what he had done to that girl* at Penn State, but no name was mentioned and the information was not reported to the police at the time. Haefner died in 2002 and there was never any evidence tying him to the crime.

Even prior to Aardsma's murder, the campus of Penn State University had numerous and persistent reports of nefarious activity. Peeping Toms and exhibitionists were reported in and around Pattee Library over the Thanksgiving holiday and campus police increased their presence as a result. The area of the Level 2 core stacks was frequently described as creepy and there was evidence of sexual trysts – some same-sex – pornographic material, and drug transactions in the area of Rows 50 and 51. Some theorists believe Aardsma may have unexpectedly interrupted such activity and was killed to ensure her silence. Given his relationship with Aardsma, his later criminal history, and his unusual behavior after the murder, perhaps it was Richard Haefner.

Miscellaneous confessions and accounts for which there is no subsequent explanation or information include a university employee that boasted about killing Aardsma at a campus party and an Art student who remarked the day after the murder that it would be simple to kill someone and get away with it. A young boy discovered a knife in the bushes outside Penn State's Recreation Hall in 1970 and the police found a smear of Aardsma's blood by a stairwell not used by the EMTs when they removed Aardsma's body. The clothes that Trooper Simmers collected on the day of the crime were submitted to the State Police crime lab sometime in 2009 to check for traces of blood and hair, but the results of any testing is unknown.

Many dozens of articles are available about the murder of Betsy Ruth Aardsma, most notably those prepared by Sascha Skucek and Derek Sherwood. These two dedicated researchers also maintain a website devoted to the crime. Penn State student filmmaker Tommy Davis produced an independent film about the murder scheduled for screening at the State Theater in February 2014, but delayed until later in the year.

Charles Nicoletti

At the age of 12, Charles Nicoletti shot and killed his father in their Chicago, Illinois home. That was the first time Nicoletti killed anyone, but not the last. As part of a Chicago gang and, later, the notorious Chicago Outfit, Nicoletti has been credited with as many as 20 mob killings, but that number is just an estimate. He also has been directly implicated in the assassination of President John F. Kennedy. The irony is that the last of the mob hits associated with Charles Nicoletti was his own.

Philip and Grace Nicoletti immigrated to the United States from Sicily in 1907 and settled in Cook County, Illinois. They had two sons, Philip and Charles, both born in Chicago. The elder Philip Nicoletti was listed in U.S. Census records as a teamster, but he was – more importantly – a mean drunk.

Fearing yet another beating from his abusive father, at 7:30 P.M. on February 25, 1929, the youngest Nicoletti son, Charles, took a pistol from a bedroom bureau drawer and shot his father, age 39, to death. Charles was 12 years old.

Charles Nicoletti was cleared of his father's death just two days later by the Cook County Coroner's Office. The Coroner determined the cause of death to be intentional homicide after the boy was threatened by his drunk, knife-wielding father. According to the Coroner's records, Charles was not only exonerated, but also commended for protecting his family.

At about age 14, Charles Nicoletti quit school and joined Chicago's notorious Forty-Two street gang. Formed in 1925, the gang would become one of the most notorious in the United States. The gang also became a steady supplier of members for the various adult crime organizations, including those run by Bugs Moran and Al Capone. At the time Nicoletti joined the 42ers, the gang already had a membership list that included notables like Sam Giancana.

Made up of young boys and men – some as young as nine years old – the 42ers were a serious thorn in the side of Chicago's police for about two decades. Operating out of the *patch* (the Little Italy section of Chicago's west side), the largely Italian juvenile gang was willing to do pretty much anything to make money. They robbed stores, stole vendor carts, killed when they needed to (including policemen), kidnapped people for ransom, and committed rape on a regular basis. With their charm and reputation, they also had a large female following. Young girls hid weapons for them under their skirts, served as lookouts during their escapades, and were always available for sex. Because the gang was intent on being noticed by Al Capone's mob, members did everything they could to get mentioned in the newspapers and, eventually, it worked.

Thinking the 42ers were too reckless and might draw unwanted attention to his mob, Capone initially hesitated to accept any of them into his organization. One of Capone's lieutenants, however – Tony Accardo – heard that one of the 42er's *smart heads* (leaders), Sam Giancana, was a good driver and made him an offer. Accardo and Paul Ricca saw Giancana as both disposable and someone who would kill for them if needed, so they took him on as a chauffeur. Giancana, then, became the first member of the 42ers to join Capone's syndicate and, within no time, was making a name for himself doing a variety of mob chores. As Giancana proved himself, he started bringing other 42ers into the organization as well. One of the first was Charles Nicoletti.

As the years passed, many of the old Capone mob either had died or were aging so, in the early 1950s, Accardo and Ricca promoted Giancana as operating head of the Capone syndicate. In turn, Giancana hired more 42ers to help with growing racketeering operations and the notorious Giancana Crime Family, or Chicago Outfit, was born.

It was during this time that Nicoletti and Phillip Alderiso came up with the concept of the *hitmobile*. Usually a dark colored sedan (stolen), the vehicle was outfitted with unique features, including three switches under the dashboard. Two of the switches disabled the taillights so that the car would be harder for police to track at night. The third switch opened hidden compartments containing brackets to which weapons of various types could be attached. The brackets were designed to hold everything from a handgun to a machine gun. Over time, the Chicago police confiscated several hitmobiles, but Nicoletti and Alderiso had already earned admiration from the organization for their creativity and just kept turning them out. From their humble beginnings as ruffian 42ers, they were on their way up the Mob ladder.

By the end of the 1960s, Nicoletti had become one of the most notorious and dangerous of Giancana's lieutenants and the FBI was watching him closely. Among the most gruesome crimes attributed to Nicoletti was the kidnapping, torture, and murder of a small-time burglar Billy McCarthy. After a bar fight, McCarthy and his cohort Jimmy Miraglia killed two Chicago Outfit members, but the name of McCarthy's accomplice was not known. To extract the accomplice's name, Nicoletti, Alderiso, and Anthony Spilotro kidnapped McCarthy and placed his head in a steel vice. Not wanting to snitch, Spilotro kept tightening the vice until one of McCarthy's eyes popped out of its socket. At that point, McCarthy provided Miraglia's name. Both McCarthy and Miraglia were found later in the trunk of a car with their throats cut.

Through the 1960s and 1970s, Giancana's organization generated incredible wealth and power for the Mob. His operations expanded into Las Vegas, Mexico, and Cuba, and the list of politicians and entertainers Giancana called *friend* was impressive. While that was appealing to many, insiders like Paul Ricca thought his activities were drawing too much unwanted attention – especially from government agencies like the IRS and CIA – so in the mid 1970s, Giancana's role in the organization was given to Joey Aiuppa, and his esteem in the Chicago Outfit plummeted. Giancana was also on the list to testify at House Select Committee on Assassinations hearings into the murder of John F. Kennedy and that made the Chicago Outfit extremely nervous.

On June 19, 1975, Sam Giancana was executed in the kitchen of his Oak Park Illinois home. He was shot 7 times in the head. His long time friend, Charles Nicoletti was furious.

Conspiracy theorists have long attempted to link President John F. Kennedy's assassination to the Chicago Crime Syndicate. Volumes have been written about this possible link, although like many other theories, there is no definitive proof. The relationship between Charles Nicoletti and this subject considers the relationship between, among others, Nicoletti, James Earl Files, Sam Giancana, Johnny Rosselli, and Lee Harvey Oswald. The convoluted theory relies heavily on a confession by Files and a package of information allegedly given to him by Nicoletti after the JFK assassination for safekeeping. When given the package, Nicoletti allegedly told Files that it might save his life one day. Files insists that the package included a map of the Dallas motorcade route and several Secret Service ID badges, which he eventually destroyed.

Although there have been inconsistencies in his confession over the years, Files states that he and Charles Nicoletti were the killers of John F. Kennedy; Lee Harvey Oswald helped with logistics and planning the week before. Nicoletti and Rosselli were positioned in the Texas Book Depository and one of them shot the President from behind. Files claims to be the long sought shooter on the grassy knoll, who was hiding behind the stockade fence near the railroad yard. He insists that he took one shot only with a Remington XP-100 Fireball rifle and that his shot – the kill shot – was simultaneous with a final shot from Nicoletti.

Files claims that there was so much confusion after the shooting that no one paid any attention to him. He put his weapon into a small case, reversed his jacket to subtly change his appearance, and simply walked away.

Governor Connolly and Jacqueline Kennedy were specifically excluded as targets; Connolly's injury was collateral damage.

James Earl Files is currently serving a 50-year sentence at the Statesville Correctional Center in Crest Hill, Illinois, for the attempted murder in 1991of two police officers.

It was well known within the Chicago Outfit, that Charles Nicoletti was extremely upset over the execution of his long time friend Sam Giancana and, after being seen (innocently) with an FBI agent, some felt he was about to become an informant. Others thought the hit ordered on Nicoletti was pay back for an unauthorized murder he was believed to have carried out in Milwaukee. Still others thought it was to keep him from testifying at the House hearings into JFK's murder. Whatever the reason, on March 29, 1977, Charles Nicoletti was found murdered in his car in a Chicago restaurant parking lot. He had three execution-style .38-caliber gunshot wounds to the back of his head. Nicoletti had become the victim of his own profession.

It is believed that Harry Aleman, a known Chicago Outfit assassin, executed Charles Nicoletti, but the exact motive is unknown and his death remains unsolved.

February 9 Killer

On February 9, 2006, and February 9, 2008, an unknown assailant committed two seemingly unrelated murders. The killings occurred just 1 mile apart. Anticipating similar crimes to occur on the same date in the following years, Utah police repeatedly warned the public and stepped up their patrols. There were no similar crimes recorded on those dates – at least not in the state of Utah – but the perpetrator of both is considered a possible serial killer after DNA testing in 2009 linked them to the same person. With no new leads, Utah police declared the crimes cold cases in 2011.

At approximately 11:30 on the morning of February 9, 2006, 29-year-old McDonald's employee Sonia Mejia was raped and fatally strangled in her apartment in Taylorsville, Utah. She was 6 months pregnant with her second son. The child did not survive the attack, making the crime a double homicide. Even seasoned police officers described the crime as horrible because the unborn child was fully developed.

After dropping her 8-year-old son at school earlier in the morning, witnesses reported seeing Mejia arguing with a young Hispanic male carrying a bag of Cheetos and a bottle of Coca Cola. The man struck her in the face at the apartment's front entrance and then pushed his way in when she tried to close the door. No one reported the attack to the police.

At 6 P.M., Mejia's husband returned from work to find his wife on the bed battered and not breathing and called the Taylorsville police. Mejia was gagged with a dark blue bandana and there was a wire around her neck; she was pronounced dead at the scene. The young mother's car keys and 1998 Ford Escort were missing, as was the jewelry she was seen wearing earlier in the day. The jewelry items were described as a heart-shaped ruby ring, a diamond ring, and a gold necklace with an *Our Lady of Guadeloupe* medallion. Police recovered the car 4 days later in a motel parking lot in Murray, Utah, approximately 12 blocks from the crime scene, but it provided no fingerprints or other forensic evidence. The jewelry was never recovered and none of the items appeared in pawnshops. Taylorsville police believe they were probably given away as gifts. Surveillance cameras located at both the motel and businesses near the apartment offered no useful clues.

From the little information known about this crime, the Taylorsville police do not believe Mejia knew her attacker. The working theory is that either the assailant was attracted to her – or she matched his profile – and that possibly he knew her schedule and followed her home.

Damiana Castillo was uncharacteristically absent from church on the morning of February 9, 2008, and the whole congregation knew something was wrong. When her 32-year-old son checked on her about 10 A.M. that morning, he found the 57-year-old grandmother dead on her West Valley City, Utah, apartment's living room floor. Castillo had been beaten and strangled and items in the apartment were moved. There was no sign of forced entry and the neighbors did not hear or see anything unusual. No one could provide a description of the assailant and the West Valley City police have offered no additional information about the crime since it was committed.

In addition to being murdered on the same date, exactly 2 years apart, both female victims were Hispanic. The two women were strangled while alone in their apartments and lived in Salt Lake City neighborhoods located a few blocks apart. Both communities are densely populated with Hispanic residents.

Although police from the two jurisdictions have declined to reveal all of the evidence, at a press conference in February 2009, they jointly announced a match in both the DNA profile and the physical description of what has become known as the *February 9 Killer*. Based on the eyewitness accounts from the Mejia murder and, possibly, the later DNA profile that matched both crimes, Taylorsville and West Valley City authorities believe the perpetrator of the two crimes was a young (late teens or early 20s) male, approximately 5-foot 3 inches to 5-foot 5 inches tall and weighing between 130 and 150 pounds. His hair was described as short, black, and combed back. At the time of the Mejia attack, he was reported to be wearing denim shorts (below-knee length), white tennis shoes (without socks), and a white T-shirt.

Working with the Federal Bureau of Investigation, Taylorsville police also believe that the suspect may have a history of animal abuse. Without matches to the killer's DNA in existing databases, the FBI has also suggested that the perpetrator is psychopathic with no criminal history. He is also likely an unregistered sex offender.

In 2010, the Salt Lake County District Attorney's Office filed charges in 3rd District Court against the *February 9 Killer*, listing him as a *John Doe* having the specific DNA profile associated with the Mejia and Castillo cases. The filing is the only known Salt Lake County homicide case moved forward using this unusual approach. The timing of the charges was primarily to avoid expiration of the statute of limitations for the homicide counts. Among the felony charges filed against *John Doe* there were two counts each of aggravated murder, aggravated burglary, aggravated robbery, and aggravated sexual assault. Because of the slaying of Mejia and her unborn child, the aggravated murder counts carry the potential penalty of death.

The two cases were officially assigned to the Taylorsville and West Valley City Cold Case divisions in 2011, but authorities in both jurisdictions continue to encourage anyone with knowledge of the crimes to come forward, including non-English-speaking residents who might be concerned with their, or a loved-ones, immigration status. Authorities have worked actively with Hispanic advocacy groups and Spanish-language television and radio stations as well stressing that they do not want residents to be afraid to come forward. In addition, Meadow Gold Dairy offered two $5,000 rewards for any information leading to the arrest and conviction of the individual associated with these crimes.

The motive for the Mejia and Castillo murders and the significance of the February 9 date, if any, remain unknown.

The Mejia and Castillo murders may be the loose inspiration for the character Johnny Ray Covey in a season eight episode of the CBS television network program *Criminal Minds*. Although the show's credits did not reference the two murders, the fictionalized murderer (Covey) targeted Hispanic women, one of whom was pregnant, and disposed of their bodies on the same day each year (May 13).

Frankford Slasher

Frankford is a neighborhood in northeast Philadelphia. Although the community once had a rich history with thriving businesses and palatial estates, by the 1980s, drugs, failing businesses, and a decades-old elevated transit system (the El) had transformed Frankford from a destination into a *ride-over* area teeming with addicts and prostitutes. Between 1985 and 1990, there was a serial killer prowling the streets and northeast Philadelphia became known nationally as the home of the Frankford Slasher. During that 5-year period, there were eight, possibly nine, bizarre and gruesome murders. Philadelphia authorities consider all but one of the crimes to be unsolved. There was a conviction in the eight crime (seventh victim), but no evidence to link the assailant to the others. There also are lingering doubts surrounding the one conviction.

All of the Frankford Strangler's murders were associated with Frankford Avenue, a busy 13-block-long strip of shops, bars, and eateries located in the shadow of Philadelphia's El. For decades, the area has been known for its nightlife and as a place where one could buy a drink anytime night or day.

Police did not see a pattern in the crimes until victim four (Jeanne Durkin), at which time they established a task force and started canvassing the Frankford Avenue neighborhoods and shop owners looking for clues to a serial killer. Authorities focused on the Golden Bar (Goldie's) in the 5200 block of Frankford Avenue, where all of the victims were either regular or occasional customers. One of the bartenders believed the killer was also a patron and provided the name of at least one man that she thought might be committing the crimes. After hundreds of interviews, 50 men matching witness descriptions and the police sketch were investigated; two suspects were placed under surveillance, but not arrested or charged.

Helen Patent was 52 years old and lived in Bucks County, Pennsylvania, with her estranged husband Kermit. Kermit later told police that he had not seen Helen since August 19 but that it was not unusual for her to be absent for long periods of time. The next time Kermit Patent would see Helen Patent would be in the Philadelphia morgue. People from the Frankford area, where she was found, were not even aware that she had a husband or home elsewhere.

Although accounts vary, newspaper articles reveal that on August 26 at about 8:30 in the morning, train yard workers stumbled on the body of a white female among rows of stacked railroad ties. The victim was nude from the waist down, posed provocatively, and had been viciously stabbed multiple times in the chest, head, and right arm. There was also a long wound to her abdomen that was so deep her internal organs were exposed. Autopsy records show that Helen Patent suffered 47 stab wounds; she had also been sexually assaulted.

According to acquaintances interviewed by the police, Patent would visit the Frankford area periodically, staying for a time and then disappearing. She frequented many of the local nightspots and bars, but was a regular at Goldie's. The bartender at Goldie's described her as street savvy, a loner, and someone who preferred to buy her own drinks. No one believed she would have voluntarily gone to the train yard with a stranger. Whether Helen Patent was a prostitute, or perceived to be by her killer, is not known.

Anna Carroll lived in south Philadelphia in the 1400 block of Ritner Street, not far from Methodist Hospital. She was 68 years old. When neighbors checked to see why her front door was open on a cold winter's day, they found her body lying on the bedroom floor. Similar to Helen Patent, Carroll was naked from the waist down and had died from multiple, although fewer (six) stab wounds, mostly to the back. Carroll also had a long, wide postmortem wound from the breastbone to the groin; a kitchen knife was left sticking in her body.

Carroll was frequently seen at the nightspots on Frankford Avenue and was a regular at Goldie's. In 2010, Carroll's granddaughter posted a message on a Philadelphia public Internet forum asking for information about her. In the message, she noted that her family had always said Anna was a hardworking woman and not a prostitute.

Susan Olszef's body was found on Christmas night 1986, at about 8:30 P.M. In circumstances nearly identical to that of Anna Carroll, Olszef lived alone in an apartment, had been stabbed six times in the back, and was found by neighbors who noticed her front door ajar. Police reported that there were no signs of forced entry.

Olszef was 64 years old and described as a small woman with bad arthritis. The bartender at Goldie's told police that Olszef, like Patent and Carroll, was a regular on Frankford Avenue and had been at Goldie's only 3 days before her murder.

The body of 28-year-old Jeanne Durkin was found by a Jerry's Restaurant worker at 7:30 in the morning of January 8, 1987. Unlike the previous victims, Durkin, the mother of four children, was homeless and had been living on or around Frankford Avenue for more than 5 years. She was most often seen by the abandoned Hanscom Bakery, two buildings from the Goldie's, where the staff occasionally let her get warm and wash up.

People who knew Jeanne Durkin told police that she had a mental condition, but that she was independent, more than strong enough to ward off an attacker, and undoubtedly knew her assailant.

Durkin's body was found in a vacant lot lying under a fruit and vegetable stand/truck. Naked from the waste down and posed provocatively, she had been savagely beaten and stabbed in the chest, buttocks, and back more than 74 times. There was a large pool of blood, and blood-spatter was found on the fruit stand and a nearby fence; she had been sexually assaulted. Lying face down, a coat had been pulled over her head.

Margaret Vaughan was found in the foyer of her apartment building on Penn Street. Age 66, Vaughan had been evicted from the building that same morning. Police reports show that Vaughan was stabbed 29 times.

An employee of Goldie's told police that Vaughan had been in the bar the night before her murder drinking with a Caucasian man who wore glasses and walked with a limp. A Philadelphia police artist produced a sketch based on the barmaid's description, but he was never identified.

The sixth victim attributed to the Frankford Strangler was Theresa Sciortino, age 30. Also a frequent customer along the Frankford Avenue strip, Sciortino lived alone in apartment 3F on Arrott Street, just three blocks from Margaret Vaughan. Like Jeanne Durkin, Sciortino had been in and out of psychiatric facilities and, at the time of her death, was receiving outpatient mental health treatment.

Sciortino's body was found by her landlord at about 12:30 A.M. after another tenant reported hearing loud thumping noises a few hours earlier. The neighbor stated that the noises sounded like a person falling, or being thrown to the floor, and were followed by someone leaving the victim's apartment. The door to Sciortino's apartment was unlocked, but the landlord had trouble entering because it was partially blocked by the body.

When she was found, Sciortino was lying face up on the apartment floor in a large pool of blood; she was completely naked except for a pair of white socks. Police described the gruesome murder scene as encompassing the entire apartment with blood spattered everywhere. As with the previous five murders, a sharp knife was used to stab Sciortino 25 times in the face, arms, shoulder, and chest. In this crime, the assailant left the bloodstained knife in the kitchen sink, along with a 3-foot-long bloody stick that had been used to sexually assault her. Police stated that the stick appeared to be part of the apartment's doorframe.

The assailant also left a bloody footprint and police found evidence of drug use. The Philadelphia Medical Examiner's office was quoted as saying there was a pattern to Sciortino's stab wounds, but would not elaborate.

At about 2 A.M. on the morning of April 29, 1990, a patrol officer checking the area because of prior burglaries found victim 7 – Carol Dowd, age 46 – in an alley behind Newman's Sea Food. The business was located at 4511 Frankford Avenue. Also a frequent patron of the Frankford Avenue strip, Dowd was described by family members as a paranoid schizophrenic who began hearing voices after her brother died. At the time of her death, she lived in a community facility a short distance from the scene of the crime.

Dowd was stabbed viciously 36 times in the chest, back, stomach, face, and neck. The stomach wound was long and deep exposing her internal organs. Unlike the previous murders, Dowd's head and face were brutally battered and her left breast was mutilated. Dowd also showed evidence of defensive wounds on her hands and her clothing and purse were found near the body. The contents of the purse were scattered, but nothing appeared to have been stolen and the police concluded that robbery was not the motive. An eyewitness saw Dowd a few hours before she was murdered walking on Frankford Avenue with an older Caucasian man.

On the same street as the murder of Theresa Sciortino and just three blocks from where Carol Dowd was found 15 months earlier, police found the body of Michelle Dehner, age 30, lying on the floor of her tiny, efficiency apartment. This victim was already known to the police, having been a potential suspect in the murder of Jeanne Durkin after the two were seen fighting over a blanket.

Known as Crazy Michelle, Dehner was described as unfriendly, unclean, and a loner with erratic behavior. Neighbors told police that she would sometimes use furniture to barricade herself in her apartment and then throw things out the window, but that mostly she spent time frequenting the Frankford Avenue bars drinking all day. Two days before her body was found, she was seen leaving the Jolly Post Tavern with a Caucasian man. It was the last time she was seen alive.

When police arrived at the murder scene on the afternoon of September 6, 1990, they found Dehner had been stabbed 23 times in the chest and stomach. The killer did not leave the murder weapon at this crime and there was no sign of forced entry.

Although the Frankford Slasher is typically credited with eight homicides, a ninth crime may also belong to the same killer. This murder occurred on January 29, 1987, just 21 days after the body of Jeanne Durkin was found. Age 29, Catherine Jones was found by a passer-by in the Northern Liberties section of Philadelphia. She had been bludgeoned to death and was found partially clothed and buried in the snow. Autopsy reports revealed her jaw was broken and her skull was crushed.

According to Jones' father, Catherine was a waitress at a restaurant near Goldie's and frequented the bars along the Frankford Avenue strip. Police saw similarities with the other eight cases, but also found inconsistencies, most notably a method of death that did not include stabbing.

Elements of the Crimes

1. All of the victims were Caucasian women.
2. All of the victims frequented the Frankford Avenue strip.

3. All of the victims were regular or occasional patrons of the Golden Bar.
4. All of the victims were homeless or welfare recipients.
4. With the exception of the possible ninth victim (Catherine Jones), all were viciously stabbed multiple times, inferring a crime of rage.
5. In most of the crimes, the women were sexually assaulted.
6. In two of the crimes, the women were also severely bludgeoned.
7. Three of the women were seen with a Caucasian man within hours of being murdered
8. Four of the women were killed outdoors; five of the women were killed in an apartment; for the inside crimes, there was no reported sign of forced entry.
9. The ages of the victims varied greatly 28 to 68 years old.
10. Given the amount of blood that must have been on the killer, no one noticed him.
11. The bloody footprint found at the Theresa Sciortino crime scene was the most promising of the clues. The manufacturer of the shoe was identified, but there were no matches to any of the men under investigation.

When victim 7, Carol Dowd, was found murdered behind Newman's Sea Food, the police questioned dozens of people in the surrounding neighborhood. Among them was 39-year-old Leonard Christopher, an African American fish cutter at Newman's, who also lived nearby. During questioning, Christopher mentioned that he had known Margaret Vaughan (victim 5). Knowing one of the earlier victims and working in the business where a second was murdered, the police immediately became suspicious and asked him for an alibi for the night that Dowd was killed.

Christopher told police that he was with his girlfriend that night, but when she was questioned, she denied they were together. Other witnesses provided conflicting stories. One placed Christopher in a bar with Dowd on the night she was killed and two Frankford Avenue prostitutes placed him first outside the bar with her and then coming from behind the fish market, sweating, and carrying a big knife.

Believing these accounts were sufficient for a search warrant, police searched Christopher's apartment and found a tiny bloodstain on a pair of his slacks. The spot was too small to test for DNA or link him to the crime. Both Christopher and his boss at the fish market said he got the speck of blood on his clothes when he was asked to clean up the alley after Dowd's murder. Several coworkers came forward to vouch for Christopher's good character, as did his landlord. Still others testified to his gentle manner and the fact that he was well liked.

Despite the fact that Christopher, who had no criminal record, did not resemble the police artist sketch or descriptions provided by several Frankford Slasher witnesses – young, tall black man vs. a short middle-aged Caucasian man with glasses and a limp – police arrested him on May 5, 1990, for the murder of Carol Dowd. He was also charged with robbery, abuse of a corpse, and possession of an instrument of a crime (the knife). Christopher was denied bail, but was not charged with any of the other murders

On September 6, 1990, while Leonard Christopher was in jail awaiting trial, Michelle Dehner was found murdered in exactly the same manner as the other Slasher crimes. The police had no explanation and refused to comment.

Initially relieved that a serial murderer had been caught, the public now feared that the real killer was still on the loose and that the Philadelphia police had the wrong man. Calls for Christopher to be released were ignored and, on November 29, 1990, he went on trial. On December 12, Leonard Christopher was found guilty of the first-degree murder of Carol Dowd and sentenced to life in prison; the prosecutor had asked for the death penalty.

According to the local newspapers, Christopher was convicted completely on hearsay. There was no evidence connecting him to the crime, no murder weapon, and conflicting accounts of several Frankford Avenue prostitutes and drug addicts. Most importantly, he was in jail at the time of the last crime. After the trial, Christopher said he had been railroaded by authorities who felt pressure to solve the crime and by *pipers* – prostitutes pressured into testifying by the police.

Leonard Christopher is currently incarcerated at the State Correctional Institute in Huntingdon, Pennsylvania. As of March 2014, his possible wrongful conviction is being investigated by attorneys with the Pennsylvania Innocence Project.

Samples from two other cases are scheduled for DNA testing, but the status of the analysis is not known.

Freeway Phantom

During a 16-month period between April 1971 and September 1972, a serial killer nicknamed the *Freeway Phantom* stalked southeast Washington D.C. The case involved the random abduction and strangulation of six young African-American girls between the ages of 10 and 18. Some of the girls were held captive for several days and four, perhaps all, were raped; all of the bodies were left near busy roadways. Multiple jurisdictions handled the investigation, but by 1973, the case had stalled. Over the next three decades, authorities made periodic attempts to solve the murders, but there was never sufficient evidence to charge anyone.

Carol Denise Spinks: The first of the *Freeway Phantom* abductions occurred on April 25, 1971. In the twilight of that evening, Carol Spinks, age 13, crossed the boundary from her home in Maryland into Washington D.C. and walked about a half mile to buy groceries at a 7-Eleven for her family's dinner. She was abducted on the way home after purchasing TV dinners, bread, and sodas. Six days later, an 11-year-old boy walking on the grassy shoulder of the northbound lanes of Interstate 295 found the child's body. Except for her shoes, she was fully clothed and had been sexually molested and strangled. Spinks was one of only two (the first two victims) whose body was found within the boundary of the District of Columbia.

Darlenia Denise Johnson: On July 8, 1971, high school senior Darlenia Johnson left her apartment about 10:30 in the morning for summer counseling job at a local recreation center. Her home was just a few blocks from where the Spinks family lived and she walked to her job along the same street where Carol Spinks was abducted. Just 16 years old, Johnson was not seen alive again. Eleven days after her abduction, an electric company lineman found Johnson's body along Interstate 295 a few feet from where Carol Spinks' body was found three months earlier. Johnson died from strangulation, although her body was badly decomposed and the police could not initially determine the cause or confirm whether she had been sexually assaulted. She was shoeless.

Brenda Fay Crockett: Nineteen days after Darlenia Johnson was abducted, Brenda Crockett, age 10, disappeared under circumstances similar to that of Carol Spinks. On the night of July 27, 1971, the young girl was sent to a northwest Washington D.C. grocery store just five blocks away by her mother; she never returned. Of the six *Freeway Phantom* cases, this crime took an unusual turn, when the child called her home 3 hours after being abducted. During the brief and tearful call, Brenda Crockett told her 7-year-old sister that she had been picked up by a white man who promised to send her home in a taxi from somewhere in Virginia. Within minutes, the child called again and repeated the story to her mother's boyfriend, adding that she was in a house with a white man. When the boyfriend asked to speak to the man, the phone line went dead. Within hours, Brenda Crockett's body was found by a hitchhiker at a Route 50 underpass, near Interstate 295 in Prince George's County, Maryland. A scarf with a knot was tied around her neck and she had been brutally raped and strangled. Like the first two victims, Crockett was shoeless. Police theorized that the child was forced by the killer to make the phone calls to confuse the investigation, possibly because an eyewitness saw her in a black car with an African-American man shortly after she was abducted.

Nenomoshia Yates: The fourth of the *Freeway Phantom's* victims was 12-year-old Nenomoshia Yates. Yates was sent to a Safeway Grocery Store in northeast Washington, D.C. about 6:30 P.M. on the night of October 1, 1971, to buy a sack of sugar. On the way home – about 7 P.M. – the child was kidnapped less than a block from the store while walking along the sidewalk. She was raped and strangled. Given the other recent abductions, her family called the police to report her missing, but it was too late. Within 3 hours, her body had been found approximately 5 miles away, next to Pennsylvania Avenue and just across the Washington D.C./Maryland border, again in Prince George's County, Maryland. The bag of sugar and the change from her purchase was found with the body. It was after this victim was found that the local media began using the nickname *Freeway Phantom*.

Brenda Denise Woodward: At 18 years old, Brenda Woodward was the oldest of the *Freeway Phantom's* victims. On November 15, 1971, Woodward and a friend left a night class from their high school in northwest Washington D.C., had dinner at a local restaurant, and, about 10:30 P.M., together took a bus to their homes in northeast Washington. Along the way, Woodward transferred to a second bus at the corner of Eighth and H Street Northeast. Six hours later, Woodward's body was found by a patrol officer near the access road leading from the Baltimore-Washington Parkway to the Prince George's County, Maryland, hospital. The body was found in a grassy area, draped with a coat; Woodward had been stabbed six times and strangled. In the pocket of the coat there was a note written in Woodward's handwriting. Later published in its entirety in the local newspapers, the message was signed *The Freeway Phantom*; however, police believe the killer dictated the taunting message, which inferred *catch me if you can*. Similar to Darlenia Johnson, Woodward had been a summer counselor at a local recreation center.

Diane Denise Williams: Diane Williams, age 17, is believed to be the final *Freeway Phantom* victim. After fixing dinner for her family on the night of September 5, 1972, the Anacostia high school senior left home to visit her boyfriend and was last seen alive as she boarded a bus for home. Williams was strangled and sexually assaulted, and her body found in Prince Georges County, Maryland, along Interstate 295 about a quarter of a mile south of the Washington D.C. border. Semen samples were collected from both the body and clothes of Diane Williams and are the only known samples remaining from the *Freeway Phantom* investigation. As of 2014 – 42 years after the crime was committed – results of DNA testing have not been released.

Several striking patterns link the six *Freeway Phantom* crimes:

- All six victims were young, African-American girls abducted within the boundary of the District of Columbia. All lived in the southeast quadrant of the District.
- Although they varied in age from 10 to 18 years old, all six girls were of similar build and physically appeared to be about the same age.
- The six girls were all strangled. Four, and likely all six, were sexually assaulted.
- The bodies of all six girls were left alongside either major Interstates or roadways – two within the District of Columbia, the remaining four in Prince George's County, Maryland.
- All six girls had synthetic green carpet fibers recovered from their bodies.
- Three of the girls lived near one another.
- All of the victims were found fully clothed; however, the first three were found shoeless.
- Four of the girls (victims 1, 2, 5, and 6) had the same middle name – Denise – and two had the same first name – Brenda.
- All six girls were alone and in clear view of public streets as they walked to or from work, school, a grocery store, or a bus stop. All six also were abducted near twilight or at night.
- Two of the girls were former recreation center counselors.

- No eyewitness saw any the abductions or any of the bodies being placed along the highway, although one eyewitness did see Brenda Fay Crockett in a dark-colored car with an African-American man.

Some of the criminal patterns parallel those of crimes committed in the same area during the same period. Correctly or incorrectly, each of the crimes not ascribed to the *Freeway Phantom* was eventually attributed to others.

Since the crimes first took place in 1971, investigators from multiple jurisdictions have interviewed hundreds of witnesses and family members and reviewed thousands of pages of police and FBI files and citizen tips. Activity on the case has waxed and waned since it first went cold in 1973, but curious and relentless detectives have periodically pursued new leads. Confounding the investigations, police procedures have changed over the intervening years and some of the original evidence has been lost or destroyed.

In 1974, the FBI and other local authorities investigated a possible connection between the six missing girls and the Green Vega Rapists – a gang of men that was abducting and sexually assaulting dozens of women across the District of Columbia. One of the gang members cooperated with the FBI, claimed to have participated in the murders of the six young girls, and accused others. In the end, he retracted his confession and no charges were filed.

In 1977, a Washington D.C. homicide detective was asked to question a rape suspect named Robert Elwood Askins to determine if there was any connection to the *Freeway Phantom* cases. Askins had a long criminal history that included multiple charges for kidnapping and rape. He also was known to use the word tantamount, an unusual word that appeared in the note that police found in Brenda Woodward's coat pocket. A search warrant was granted for Askins' home and property and the police physically dug up Askins' back yard, but no evidence to link him to the crimes could be found and no charges were filed. A *Washington Post* reporter contacted Askins in 2006 while he was serving a life sentence at the Federal Correctional Institution in Cumberland, Maryland, for kidnapping and rape, but Askins denied the killings right up until his death in prison in 2010.

In April 2006, the Major Case/Cold Case Unit of the Metropolitan Police Department and the Prince George's County, Maryland, Police Homicide Unit distributed a $150,000 reward poster with photographs of all six victims to encourage tips. No one has come forward.

Some of the authorities who have followed this case for the last four decades believe the *Freeway Phantom* was clever enough not to be caught; others think he was just lucky.

Goleta Serial Killings

He always struck between 9 P.M. and 7 A.M. His first crime probably occurred as early as 1974 and his last in 1986. He is variously known as the Goleta Serial Killer, the East Side Rapist, the East Area Rapist, the Original Night Stalker (as opposed to Richard Ramirez, who was the other Night Stalker), the Diamond Knot Killer, the Bedroom Killer, and the Golden State Killer. Most law enforcement officials simply call him EAR/ONS; some believe he is also the infamous Visalia Ransacker. Despite the many names, the unidentified man associated with them is the same person and, perhaps, the most active, depraved serial criminal of the 20th century.

While violent crimes have been linked to him in and around Goleta, California, 10 or more savage murders and more than 50 rapes were committed by the East Area Rapist/Original Night Stalker (EAR/ONS) across Santa Barbara, Sacramento, Contra Costa, Ventura, Orange, and very likely Tulare counties. Excluding the probable connection between EAR/ONS and scores of crimes associated with the Visalia Ransacker, the 10-year-long violent crime spree began in October 1975, when eight rapes occurred within a year. Although it is impossible to confirm, his last known crime was in 1986 with the brutal bludgeoning of a woman in Irvine. Methods used by the criminal and DNA analysis have linked the earliest crimes with the later crimes and many that occurred in between. As of 2014, authorities still have not identified the killer who terrorized six California counties.

After nearly 40 years, law enforcement personnel from various jurisdictions have formed a consistent profile of EAR/ONS. The profile is based on eyewitness accounts, victim descriptions, methods and weapons used during the assaults, confirmed

DNA links across the locations and crimes, and psychological sketches developed by various experts.

According to police records and newspaper accounts during and after his crime spree, EAR/ONS would watch homes, usually in upscale neighborhoods, for some period before the crime. Evidence of forced entry was not always found; however, he sometimes used a screwdriver to force open sliding glass doors or entered the home ahead of the crime to loosen window screens for later visits. To avoid having his car identified, he parked well away from the intended crime scene, sometimes stealing a bicycle for the hurried return.

His earlier crimes focused on women living alone. When that detail was released to the media, he escalated to couples. Both victims would be tied up using a distinctive diamond-shaped knot and the man would be threatened with the woman's death if he attempted in any way to prevent the rape. Before and after the crime, EAR/ONS often made threatening calls to his victims, but the calls were always too short to be traced. A recording of at least one of the calls is among the evidence files. Many of the victims appeared to have been targeted rather than chosen at random.

As a nocturnal assailant, EAR/ONS slipped quietly into bedrooms, shining a flashlight at the victims. He then threatened them with a gun or knife, bound them with pre-cut items brought to the scene, and typically placed the couples in separate rooms. While in the home, he continuously yelled at them for money and jewelry. His most unusual quirk was to place dishes or similar items on the man's back, threatening death if he heard them rattle.

Profiled as psychopathic or paranoid schizophrenic, after assaulting his victims, he was occasionally heard to be crying and muttering about his mother. At one crime scene, he stopped in the middle of the rape to eat apple pie. In December 1977, he reportedly sent a poem to Sacramento news bureaus comparing himself to Jesse James and the Son of Sam.

Having been seen by several witnesses, a sketch of EAR/ONS was distributed to the media before his crimes escalated to murder, but there were no leads. After release of the sketch, the crimes appeared to have stopped, but in actuality, he had simply moved his activities to the southern part of the state, where he committed additional rapes and murders in Orange County.

In 1986, the killer's crime streak stopped as unexpectedly as it began. California law enforcement officials monitored other parts of the country for similar patterns, but found none.

Physical, Psychological, and Methodological Characteristics

- Blood Type: A positive (non-secretor)
- Build/Race/Age: athletic white male between the ages of 19 and 30 at the time the crimes began
- Clothing: usually, but not always, wore a bandana or fabric ski-type mask (various colors), dark clothes, and gloves
- Crime Scene Preferences: upscale neighborhoods; bedrooms/beds; darkness.
- Distinguishing Features: possible tattoo of a bull on his left or right forearm; small penis. There are discrepancies in hair color and length, although several witnesses described it as light in color and shoulder length.
- Eyes: blue or hazel
- Height: between 5-foot 7 inches and 5-foot 11 inches

- Intellect: knowledgeable about police procedures and various types of security devices (e.g., avoidance of, or ability to disable, security systems and locks)
- Kill Methods: bludgeoning to death with household items (e.g., fireplace log, pipe wrench, or other unrecovered blunt instrument); execution-style shooting, especially for those he did not think he could control.
- Miscellaneous: sometimes accompanied by a German shepherd dog.
- Sexual Tendencies: despite the presence of semen, not all of the victims were sexually assaulted.
- Shoe Size/Type: 9-91/2; tennis shoes; military-type boots; hiking boots
- Voice: high-pitched and raspy; spoke with clenched teeth
- Weapons and Tools: typically armed with a flashlight, a hand gun (.38-, .45-, or .357-caliber), a stick, a club, and/or a knife. Victim's were tied with shoestrings or pre-cut shipping or drapery twine or nylon cord brought to the crime scene by the killer
- Weight: 150 to 170 pounds.

The EAR/ONS crimes in Goleta began October 1, 1979. The first of the crimes occurred at the home of Abraham Himmel and Jennifer Horniek. Awakened by a flashlight in their faces at 2 A.M., the two 33-year-old computer programmers were tied up in separate rooms. Horniek was bound and left on the floor of the living room with her tennis shorts used as a blindfold. Himmel was bound and left in the bedroom. While the intruder was muttering to himself and fumbling through items in the kitchen, Horniek was able to untie her feet and run screaming out the front door. In the confusion, Himmel hopped into the back yard and hid behind a tree. An eyewitness described the suspect as a thin male riding away on a bicycle. Both of the victims escaped physically unharmed, but badly shaken. The first of three crimes in the same neighborhood, police later believed that the attack was a test run, or practice murder, that went awry.

The second Goleta attack took place on December 30, 1979, less than a half mile from the first. The victims were a surgeon, Dr. Robert Offerman (age 44), and his 35-year-old psychologist girlfriend Debra Alexandria Manning. Both were found naked in the master bedroom with their hands bound behind them – Manning on the waterbed and Offerman on his knees on the floor. Manning had been shot once in the back of the head with a .38-caliber pistol; Offerman had three gunshot wounds to the back and one gunshot wound to the chest. Pry marks were on the door and windowsills, and size 9 tennis shoe prints were found around the home. A pre-cut length of nylon cord was tied around Offerman's wrist, and police later revealed that the suspect was accompanied by a dog. Large dog prints were seen in the muddy backyard. Before leaving the residence, the suspect went to the refrigerator, ate the remains of the couple's Christmas turkey, and discarded the remains on the patio. The coroner set the time of death for both victims at 3 A.M.

The day prior to the second Goleta murders, there were also five Goleta area burglaries. Four of the home invasions involved sliding glass doors being pried open. At one of the crime scenes, a family returned home to find their dog had been beaten to death.

Goleta crime number three occurred on July 26, 1981. The victims were Gregory Sanchez (age 27) and Cheri Domingo (age 35), who were killed when they were housesitting near the Offerman condominium. Both victims were nude, Domingo on the bed and Sanchez near the bedroom closet. Domingo died of a single blunt-force blow to the head. Sanchez was shot in the face, but it was not a fatal wound. He subsequently suffered 24 blunt-force wounds to the head. There was no evidence of forced entry, but a small window screen had been removed. Several neighbors reported seeing the suspect with a German shepherd dog earlier in the evening. The description matched many given of EAR/ONS over the years.

DNA analysis conducted in 2011 matched evidence from all three of the Goleta crimes well as to two murders in Ventura and two murders in Laguna Niguel. All of the crimes are linked to the same suspect – EAR/ONS, whose DNA also has been found at the crime scenes of dozens of sexual assaults across the state.

If, as many believe, this serial offender is also the Visalia Ransacker, his crime spree actually began in April 1974. In that month, the town of Visalia, California – about 240 miles south of Sacramento – experienced a series of unusual home invasions. In each case, the home was ransacked, but very little of value was ever taken. In later crimes, he specifically asked for money and jewelry, but he generally ignored cash, focusing more on sentimental items such as rings or family photographs for his souvenirs. Between April 6, 1974 and August 31, 1975, approximately 85 of these odd burglaries took place with no one seriously injured or killed.

On the night of September 11, 1975, an unidentified man attempted to kidnap a teenage girl from a home in south-central Visalia and, when confronted, shot and killed her father, College of the Sequoia's Journalism Professor Claude Snelling. Although out of character, the attempted kidnapping and murder was linked to the Visalia Ransacker by crime scene evidence. After this deviation in the Ransacker's pattern, the seemingly harmless home invasions resumed for about three months (about 10 additional crimes). On December 10, 1975, the Ransacker returned to a neighborhood of his previous crimes and was confronted by a police detective assigned to stakeout homes on the street. Startled by the detective, the Ransacker shot at but did not injure him and escaped over a backyard fence.

In 1977, the Visalia Police Department coordinated with the Sacramento County Sheriff's Department hoping to find links between a series of 23 violent rapes in Sacramento that took place between the killing of Professor Snelling and the shooting of the detective in Visalia. Although physical descriptions of the man and the methods used were very similar, there was no DNA analysis available at that time and a link to the increasingly violent crimes could not be confirmed. By the time the Ransacker's crime spree ended – or escalated to more violent crimes – he had committed more than 120 home invasions.

Hoping for a match to the Visalia burglaries, the Goleta and Irvine murders, and many other unsolved violent crimes committed across California since 1977, investigators from the Orange County Sheriff's Department attempted (in 2000) to obtain DNA samples from 60 inmates on San Quentin's death row. The effort was derailed by a January 1997 Sacramento Superior Court-ordered injunction that prevents authorities from collecting samples from California inmates on death row. The injunction has been appealed on several occasions, but remains in force.

After DNA testing in 2001 matched the EAR/ONS to six Southern California murders committed between 1980 and May 1986, the Orange County Sheriff's Department released an FBI Violent Criminal Apprehension Program (VICAP) Alert providing specific suspect information. The alert produced no solid leads.

California voters approved an initiative in 2004 that requires the collection of DNA samples from anyone arrested for, or convicted of, a felony. The database may eventually reveal a match to EAR/ONS, but there are many thousands of samples that have not yet been entered.

Santa Barbara County Sheriff's detectives revisited evidence from numerous EAR/ONS crime scenes in 2011, and used evolving technologies to isolate traces of paint. The paint is now linked to at least two of the rapes and one of the homicides, including the 1981 double murder in Goleta. Authorities believe the perpetrator may have been a painter who worked on the Calle Real Shopping Center construction site in Goleta – a project that was permitted to a developer from Sacramento. In September 2013, this information was released to the media in hopes that someone would have knowledge of the project and its workers.

As of 2014, there are multiple blood, semen, and hair samples on file for EAR/ONS, but the DNA profile does not match any known dataset. If the killer is still alive, he would be between 60 and 70 years old.

Honolulu Strangler

From May 1985 to April 1986, the normally tranquil shores of Oahu, Hawaii, were terrorized by a series of killings. The crime spree began and ended abruptly, but before it was over, five women were dead. Accustomed to big-city crime, but completely unprepared for a serial killer, the Honolulu police set up a 27-person task force and enlisted support from the FBI to develop a profile of the killer. Hawaii authorities also consulted the experienced Green River Task Force, which was investigating a string of killings at about the same time. The Green River Killer was eventually caught and imprisoned for life; the Honolulu Strangler was not.

With the help of the Federal Bureau of Investigation's Behavioral Science Unit, Honolulu police developed a profile of the Honolulu Strangler that focused on Caucasian males between their late thirties and early forties, living or working near the Honolulu Airport. Profilers also believed the murders were crimes of opportunity – women alone, vulnerable, in exposed settings – and that the killer was not watching or stalking them before the crime. Considering the killer's possible motives, the FBI added that the assailant might be having problems in his relationship with a wife or girlfriend.

Based on eyewitness accounts, the killer was also thought to be driving a light-colored van with writing on the rear doors.

Semen samples taken from the victims contained few or no sperm, inferring that the suspect had probably had a vasectomy.

There were both similarities and differences among the crimes. All five were strangled with their hands bound behind them and each was found near the water. Although details from the five crimes are not complete, it is also believed that each was sexually assaulted.

Other than being Caucasian, the five women were not similar in physical appearance, indicating that the assailant was not targeting victims because of statue, hair color, or age. Robbery did not appear to be a motive and none of the women had any connection to the other.

First to Die: May 30, 1985: Still wearing the yellow jumpsuit, red belt, and jewelry she wore to go clubbing in Waikiki with friends the night before, Vicki Gail Purdy, age 25, was the Honolulu Strangler's first victim. The wife of an Army helicopter pilot, Purdy was last seen around midnight on May 29 in the parking lot of the Shorebird Hotel. When she did not respond to repeated pager messages, her husband searched for, and eventually found, her car the following morning abandoned in the parking lot of the hotel. The car had been newly dented – perhaps the method by which the killer confronted his victims. Within hours, her strangled body was found on an embankment of the Keehi Lagoon with her hands tied behind her back. With no previous crime pattern and as the first victim, police initially thought the murder was linked to her job at a video-rental store, where two women had been stabbed to death the previous year.

Physical Description: Blond hair, 5-foot 5 inches, approximately 135 pounds.
Residence: Mililani

Youngest to Die: January 15, 1986: Regina Sakamoto was a 17-year-old Leilehua High School student. On the morning of her disappearance, she missed the bus to school. Knowing she would be late, she called her boyfriend from a telephone booth about 7:15 A.M., and was never heard from again. The young girl's body was found the following day, also in the Keehi Lagoon, near the Honolulu Airport's reef runway. Sakamoto was wearing a blue tank top and white sweatshirt, but was naked from the waist down. Investigators determined that she had been raped and strangled and her hands were tied behind her. Sakamoto was the youngest of the five to die. The similarity of the Purdy and Sakamoto murders did not escape the Honolulu police, but they were not yet thinking about a possible serial killer.

Physical Description: Dark blond hair, 4-foot 11 inches, approximately 105 pounds.
Residence: Waipahu

Victim Three: February 1, 1986: The third victim of the Honolulu Strangler was Denise Hughes, age 21. Hughes was the wife of a Pearl Harbor sailor and worked as a secretary at a long-distance telephone company. Like Sakamoto, Hughes used the bus to travel to and from work. Uncomfortable waiting alone for long periods, Hughes made a point to walk to the Pearl City bus stop just before the bus arrived. It is likely that is where she was abducted. When she uncharacteristically failed to report to work on the morning of January 30, 1986, Hughes was reported missing. On February 1, three youths fishing in the Moanalua Stream discovered her body wrapped in a blue plastic tarp; she was wearing a blue dress and had been strangled and sexually assaulted; her hands were bound behind her.

On February 5, the Honolulu police realized they had a serial killer on the loose and set-up a task force for investigating the crimes.

Physical Description: Curly brown, shoulder-length hair; 5-foot 8 inches, approximately 154 pounds.
Residence: Pearl City

Victim Four: April 2, 1986: On the night of March 26, 1986, after returning from Kauai, where she had gone for the reading of her mother's will, Louise Medeiros, age 25, arrived at Honolulu Airport and walked to a bus stop. Between the airport and her home in Waipahu, the fourth victim of the Honolulu Strangler disappeared. The unemployed, single mother had been warned by family members not to take the bus at night, but the warnings went unheeded. On April 2, Medeiros' body was found by a road-paving crew below a Waipahu highway overpass and near the Waikele Stream. Wearing only the red and white flowered blouse she had worn on the airplane from Kauai, she had been murdered by strangulation and raped. As with the first three victims, her hands were tied behind her back. She was three months pregnant.

After this murder, the Honolulu police set up a series of sting operations using undercover policewomen. The sting sites were in the vicinity of the airport and Keehi Lagoon, but the killing spree was not over. A $25,000 reward sponsored by local businessmen was posted by the Honolulu Police Department, but went unclaimed.

Physical Description: 5-foot 4 inches, approximately 90 pounds.
Residence: Waipahu

Last to Die: May 3, 1986: Linda Pesce, age 36, was the last known and oldest of the Honolulu Strangler's victims. At about 6:30 P.M. on the night of April 29, Pesce left her job as a sales representative for the McCaw Telepage Company in Kakaako, but never arrived at her home. The following morning, her roommate reported her missing and by that afternoon police had located her car parked near the airport along the Nimitz Highway-H1 viaduct. Her car was seen at 7 P.M. the night before in the same location and with the emergency flashers on. A Caucasian man and a light-colored cargo van with writing on the rear doors were seen with the victim. Pesce's nude body was found on Sand Island on May 3rd. As with the other victims, she had been sexually assaulted and strangled with her hands tied behind her back.

Unlike the first four victims, the body of Linda Pesce was not inadvertently found by strangers. Instead, police were contacted by a man indicating he had been told by a psychic that her body was on Sand Island. The man – a 43-year-old Caucasian mechanic from Ewa Beach – took police to the exact location reportedly given to him by the psychic, but no body was found. Somewhat suspicious of the informant, the police searched the entire island and eventually found Pesce's remains about 150 yards away.

Physical Description: Brown hair, 5-foot 4 inches, approximately 146 pounds.
Residence: Moanalua

On May 9, just one week after the fifth victim was found, police detained the informant who came forward in the Pesce case and subjected him to about 10 hours of interrogation. He was also polygraphed and failed. The questioning did not yield a confession, but the police believed he was the serial killer and placed him under surveillance. Police were also granted a warrant to search his home in Ewa Beach and the airport cargo company where he worked, both of which were within the killing zone. Investigators found no evidence to tie him to the crimes.

While being observed, the man – whose name was concealed from the public – was seen driving a light-colored cargo van like the one described by the Pesce eyewitnesses. He was also observed removing the lettering from its rear doors. The woman who was an eyewitness in the Pesce case was able to pick the suspect from a photo line-up, but refused to testify, fearing for her safety.

Interviews with the man's ex-wife and girlfriend revealed that he frequently tied their hands behind their backs during sexual activity in an identical way to the five victims. The girlfriend also stated that on each of the nights that the women were murdered, she had argued with the suspect and he had left the house – possibly the trigger for the killings.

There were no known additional murders using the same methods after the Pesce homicide. Despite the circumstantial evidence amassed against the suspect, the Honolulu District Attorney's Office did not feel there was enough evidence to arrested or charge him in the five homicides. Shortly after being questioned, the suspect left Hawaii, but as a possible serial killer, his whereabouts continued to be monitored by the Honolulu Police until he died in 2005. Investigators hoped to obtain DNA samples to link the suspect to the crimes, but the results of that effort are not known.

Mary S. Sherman

Mary Stults Sherman was born on April 21, 1913, in Evanston, Illinois, and died on July 21, 1964, in New Orleans, Louisiana. Sherman earned a medical degree in 1941 and, by 1952, had been appointed laboratory director at the prestigious Ochsner Clinic Medical Foundation in New Orleans. That Dr. Sherman was a brilliant scientist and cancer researcher is not in dispute. The circumstances surrounding her work and bizarre death are quite another matter and filled with unresolved questions, tales of conspiracy, and possible links to the John F. Kennedy assassination. Both the back-story of Sherman's years in New Orleans and her untimely death contain speculative information that remains unproven.

As early as the 1940s, Dr. Mary Sherman was studying viruses and publishing academic papers on her research. She was particularly interested in botanical viruses living in soils. After Sherman completed a residency in orthopedic surgery at the University of Chicago (in 1947), Dr. Alton Ochsner invited her to join his renowned clinic in New Orleans as a partner and provided her with her own cancer laboratory. Given the reputation of Dr. Ochsner and his facility, she did not hesitate and was soon on the staff of several local hospitals and the faculty at Tulane Medical School. Sherman quickly earned the reputation of an outstanding researcher and was appointed chairman of the Pathology Committee of the American Academy of Orthopedic Surgeons. Until her death in 1964, Sherman specialized in bone and soft tissue cancers.

There are those who believe that Dr. Mary Sherman and an associate, David Ferrie, who worked at a second medical facility in New Orleans, were conducting more than routine medical research. The belief is that both were working on secret projects, perhaps for the Central Intelligence Agency or other U.S. Intelligence organizations. More specifically, believers of this theory contend that Sherman and Ferrie were developing a vaccine to prevent an epidemic of soft tissue cancers in humans from polio vaccine contaminated with Simian vacuolating virus 40 (SV-40).

In the early years of developing polio vaccine, kidney cells from monkeys were used in the process and cultures of those cells (reportedly) were found to contain SV-40. While largely dormant in the monkeys themselves, it was eventually discovered that SV-40 could produce a variety of tumors, particularly in individuals (animals or humans) with compromised immune systems. These theorists further believe that the contaminated serum was not discovered until half had already been given to the public. Unwilling to admit the problem, the makers of the vaccine supposedly distributed the second half as well – in all about 100 million doses. Data collected on the incidence of cancer in the years following administration of the contaminated vaccine apparently showed a dramatic increase in soft tissue cancers and indicated that the virus also could be passed to subsequent generations.

Sherman and Ferrie's job was to use a particle accelerator to mutate the virus and render it harmless, but instead, the virus became far more aggressive. Because the mutated virus would be of no value in offsetting the effects of the contaminated polio vaccine, the researchers supposedly tested the serum on a group of inmates at a Louisiana prison to determine its lethality. Results of the test allegedly showed that the new transmuted virus would kill a human within 28 days and could be used as a clandestine weapon that would be essentially untraceable. As proposed by several conspiracy theorists, the target for this new viral weapon was Fidel Castro. By some accounts, Mary Sherman provided medical care to exiled Cubans intending to overthrow Castro and financially supported those efforts.

In the 1980s, scientists found a batch of 1950s-era polio vaccine in a laboratory freezer. After testing, the scientists alleged that none of the samples had DNA markers consistent with known monkey viruses, thereby discrediting the polio vaccine theory. This account is unconfirmed.

Edward Haslam's book *Dr. Mary's Monkey: the Link between Polio Vaccines, Cancer, and JFK's Murder* carries the conspiracy theories about Mary Sherman's death even further. In the book, Haslam, who has extensively researched Sherman's death, names Lee Harvey Oswald as the bodyguard and handler of one of the New Orleans cancer researchers (probably Sherman) and points to David Ferrie as a co-conspirator (a get-away pilot recruited because of his years in the Civil Air Patrol) with Oswald in the John F. Kennedy assassination. Haslam further believes that Ferrie took over Sherman's research after her death and transported the weaponized polio virus to Haiti where it subsequently became the source of the AIDS and soft tissue cancer epidemics seen in subsequent decades. In 1967, David Ferrie was found dead in his apartment. Although the coroner ruled the cause of death as natural, the circumstances were suspicious. Inasmuch as he was under investigation for his possible role in the JFK assassination, some accounts indicate he may have committed suicide.

At 4:25 A.M. on the morning of July 21, 1964, the New Orleans Fire Department responded to a fire at Apartment J in the Patio Apartments at 3101 St. Charles Avenue. On entry, fire officials found no active fire anywhere in the apartment, only the smoldering body of a woman in her bed. Immediately recognizing that this was not a simple case of smoking in bed, the fire department called New Orleans police.

In the bedroom, homicide detectives found the burned body of a white female, later identified as Dr. Mary Sherman. As described in the homicide report, Sherman was nude and stretched out on her back. Clothes had been placed on top of her body, some of which were burned, others only singed. While part of her body had been severely burned, the hair on her head remained untouched.

The right side of Mary Sherman's body, from the waist to the shoulder and including her right arm and rib cage, was completely missing (possibly disintegrated by the fire) and her internal organs were visible. The left side of her body was intact, but there were several stab wounds to the left arm and another in the right leg just above the knee. Autopsy results indicated a stab wound to the heart with a very thin instrument, multiple stab wounds to the abdomen, and lacerations on the genitalia. The Medical Examiner reported the stab wound to the heart hemorrhaged, indicating that she was still alive when that wound was inflicted, but there was minimal blood at the crime scene. The remaining stab wounds were made by a heavier knife and showed no sign of hemorrhaging; they were recorded as postmortem events. A butcher knife found in the apartment was believed to be the heavier weapon, but had no useable fingerprints. Toxicology tests showed high levels of morphine in Sherman's blood.

The front door of Sherman's apartment was forced open, her wallet was empty, and her car was missing, but was found later the same day about seven blocks away. A palm print was recovered from the car, but it was too smudged to be useful. There was no sign of a struggle and the apartment did not appear to have been ransacked, although some effort had been made to open her jewelry box. Neighbors did not hear or see anything unusual.

The exact details of Sherman's missing right arm were never released to the public. Conspiracy theorists insist that the dramatic injuries to the right side of Sherman's body could not possibly have been caused by a small smoldering fire. Their belief is that she suffered a nonlethal accident, or an act of sabotage, with the particle accelerator and, rather than seeking medical care where questions would be asked, she was subsequently stabbed in the heart (the fatal wound) by a colleague and moved late at night to her apartment. The post mortem stab wounds and small mattress fire were designed to cover up her injuries and avoid explanation of Sherman's secret research. Edward Haslam and others, including investigators Philip Coppens and Joan Mellen, are convinced that Sherman was silenced because of her relationship with Lee Harvey Oswald and what she knew about the polio vaccine, the JFK assassination, and the plot to kill Castro.

At the time of her death, and to this day, police have no clues as to who killed Mary Sherman.

McStay Family Murder

In the early months of 2010, the disappearance of the McStay family from Fallbrook, California, captivated news headlines across the country. At the request of a family friend, 6 days after the family vanished, San Diego County Sheriff's deputies went to the home to investigate. Seeing nothing suspicious, they left. Three days later, the brother of the missing father climbed through an unlocked window of the home and, fearing the worst, called the deputies again. Eleven days after the family was last seen or heard from, deputies returned to the residence. They found no signs of forced entry or struggle, but food left spoiling on the kitchen counter and untended pets in the backyard showed the family left in a hurry.

In November 2013, an off-road motorcyclist found two shallow graves in the desert near Victorville, California. Forensics testing verified that the remains were from all four missing family members.

Until the evening of February 4, 2010, Joseph and Summer McStay and their two young sons Gianni (age 4) and Joseph Jr. (age 3) appeared – at least outwardly – to be living a normal southern California life. The family had recently moved from a small apartment in San Clemente to a larger home in Fallbrook, with hopes to make some upgrades, resell it, and then return to the coast. Joseph's business was building and installing decorative fountains. The business appeared to be doing well and had just been awarded a lucrative foreign contract. Fallbrook neighbors believed the family was happy and enjoying their new life.

Phone and text messages, computer traces, and credit card receipts from the day the family vanished showed no signs of stress. Summer bought toys for the children and gifts for her sister's new baby. Summer (age 43) spoke with her sister by phone that morning and Joseph (age 40) discussed business with his partner, Chase Merritt, several times during the day.

Around noon, Joseph drove to Rancho Cucamonga in the family's white Isuzu Trooper for a business lunch with Merritt; the meeting lasted about 1 hour.

At 4:25 P.M., the last outgoing phone call from the McStay's home phone was made to Joseph's cell phone and, at 5 P.M. and 5:47 P.M., Joseph and Summer McStay exchanged text messages.

Footage from security cameras belonging to a neighbor showed the Isuzu Trooper leaving their street at 7:47 P.M., but did not actually capture the occupants. Joseph used his cell phone to call Merritt about 8:28 P.M. – presumably to discuss work – and cell phone records indicate he was calling from a cell phone tower near the Old Bonsall Bridge. Merritt stated he was watching a movie and did not answer the phone.

No one in the McStay family was ever heard from again nor were there any verified sightings of them. Until their bodies were found, the San Diego County Sheriff's Office treated the McStay family disappearance as a missing person's case, even though missing person's cases involving an entire family is quite rare.

Although there are others, the most prominent of the theories regarding the disappearance and eventual murder of the McStay family are described below. As of March 2014, all of the theories are unproven. Recent remarks floating around the Internet that an arrest is imminent are speculation.

According to interviews given to various publications, the McStays may have had a history of personal debt going back as far as the 1990s. Rumors of the debt involved unsettled accounts with vendors and customers of Joseph's businesses, small claims issues, and potential problems with bankruptcy. After their disappearance, letters from various debt collectors and the Internal Revenue Service also surfaced.

The family also was rumored to be under threat of eviction from their San Clemente apartment for always being behind in their rent, yet they purchased a $320,000 home in Fallbrook just 2 months before they disappeared and had $100,000 in a personal bank account. Both Joseph and Summer's parents deny that debt has a connection to their murder. The $100,000 in their bank account has remained untouched.

In the months before the McStays disappeared, Summer used the family computer to search various Internet websites for Spanish-language software. On January 27, 2010, just 8 days before they disappeared, the same home computer was used to research passport requirements for children visiting Mexico. According to her sister, Summer's passport had expired.

At about 7 P.M. on the night of February 8, a man and woman, each holding the hand of a small boy and roughly matching the description of Joseph and Summer McStay, were captured on grainy surveillance footage crossing the Mexican border at San Ysidro (San Diego). Their white Isuzu Trooper was later found in a San Ysidro shopping center parking lot; it had been there since about 6 P.M. that same night. Reportedly, Joseph's asthma medicine was in the car – something his mother stated he would not leave behind – and there were no child car seats.

The San Diego police estimate the probability that the footage shows the family at about 75 percent; family members insist that the features and body language of the four is not a good match. Joseph's father is also certain that the family was too worried about the safety of the children to walk into Mexico at night with their two young sons.

Authorities notified Interpol to be on the lookout for the family in Mexico and asked Mexican authorities to monitor airports and bus stations. There was one possible sighting of the family by a restaurant worker in El Rosario, who accurately described the birthmark on the youngest child's forehead, but the identification could not be confirmed.

Because of potential international implications, the San Diego County Sheriff's Department officially transferred the McStay case to the FBI in San Diego in April 2013.

Although continuing to believe that the family voluntarily walked away from their life, authorities were willing to concede they may have crossed into Mexico innocently and then met with foul play. Some have speculated that the family disappeared because of a bad business deal and were later murdered by members of a Mexican cartel or other criminal organization; however, there is no evidence to indicate the McStays had any ties to the illegal drug trade.

The question of where the McStays were for the four days between 8:28 P.M. on February 4 – the night they vanished – and the time they supposedly walked across the border on February 8, is unresolved. Some believe that the family had already been murdered and that the video of them crossing the border was a different family or the crossing was staged.

Although unlikely, there are also a few researchers and amateur sleuths who think the family was placed into a Federal Witness Protection Program after either witnessing, or being a party to, a high value incident or crime. The validity of this conspiracy-type theory would necessarily assume that the four bodies found in the shallow graves near Victorville, California, were staged and not the McStays.

Summer McStay's remains were found along with the rest of the family. Associating Summer with the crime is tenuous at best, but various investigators have raised some interesting questions about her background. Over the years, she has been known by at least six aliases. She also claimed to be 10 years younger than her actual age. Chase Merritt, as well as Richard (Rick) Baker, a former San Diego-area radio personality who knew the family have both stated that Summer had a volatile temper and Merritt wrote in a recent book that Joseph suffered from an unexplained illness and thought Summer might have been trying to poison him.

While authorities have no evidence that Summer was involved in the disappearance or death of her family, they acknowledge that some of the information about her past may be relevant to the crime. Her family insists that she simply had a quirky personality.

The first person to report the McStays missing and the last known non-family member to see Joseph alive was Joseph's business partner, 57-year-old Charles (Chase) Ray Merritt. According Joseph's father, Merritt also was a trusted family friend.

A metalworker and welder, Merritt's past contains various skirmishes with the law between 1977 and 2001. Although none of his crimes have been violent, they include burglary (two charges), receiving stolen property (three charges), petty theft (one charge), criminal trespassing (one charge), grand theft (one charge), and several parole violations and citations for driving on a suspended license. Some of the crimes resulted in felony convictions and prison time. Having lived for extended periods in the Victorville area, Merritt also would be familiar with the location where the graves were found.

Theory 4 considers the possibility that Merritt alone, or with others, may have some responsibility for this crime, although a motive is unclear. Merritt was questioned by authorities and given a polygraph test that he passed. He denies involvement and has not been named a suspect in the case. As of March 2014, the McStay family is willing to give Merritt benefit of the doubt – largely because of the close relationship he had with Joseph.

In 2004, and prior to marrying Joseph McStay, Summer Martelli lived in Big Bear Lake, California, with her boyfriend Vick Wyatt Johansen. During their stormy life together, Johansen demonstrated erratic behavior, served time in jail, and was required by the courts to enter an anger management program. After the couple parted, and even after Summer married Joseph McStay and had two children, Johansen continued to contact her, believing she was his true soul mate. Six weeks before the family disappeared, Johansen sent an email to Summer professing his love and, at some point, he moved to San Clemente, about two miles from the apartment where they lived before moving to Fallbrook. On January 10, 2010, just 3 weeks before the family disappeared, Johansen was arrested at the OC Tavern for interfering with a business and resisting a peace officer. The tavern was next door to an office building that Joseph McStay had leased for his business.

After the McStays vanished, Johansen moved to Mono County, California, where he committed a string of crimes, including felony vandalism, threats against a bank teller, and breaking the window of a bar in Mammoth Lakes. After spending time in the Mono County Jail in Bridgeport, Johansen was released on probation, but it was revoked in July 2013 after he violated the terms and returned to the same bank where he had threatened the teller.

McStay family members believe Johansen's obsession with Summer, his violent behavior, and his actions around the time the family disappeared is highly suspicious. Authorities are aware of Johansen and his history, but have not commented.

Daniel Kavanaugh was the Webmaster for Joseph McStay's business. His role was to use his Internet skills to drive business to Joseph's website. At the time the McStays vanished, Kavanaugh was in Hawaii on a surfing vacation. Reportedly, many people saw him there and an online itinerary shows him on Oahu from January 4 to February 17, 2010.

To keep the company running after Joseph disappeared, Kavanaugh admits to transferring large sums of money from the business account to himself shortly after the family vanished. The withdrawals began on February 6 – just 2 days after the family disappeared, but before they were reported missing – and stopped in March 2010, when the account was frozen by the bank. Kavanaugh insists that the withdrawals were made with the consent of Joseph's brother and mother and that all of it went to various suppliers. Emails sent to Joseph during the early days of his unexplained absence were later retrieved and verified the money transfers – in total about $24,000.

In July 2011, Kavanaugh sold Joseph's company, something that Joseph's father claims he had no authority to do. Kavanaugh disagrees, stating that Joseph was the company's figurehead, but he [Kavanaugh] actually built the business.

According to public records, Kavanaugh has had skirmishes with the law. Although he claims he is not a violent person, in August 2011, he was charged with five misdemeanor counts of domestic violence and in July and received 3 years probation. In July 2013, he was charged with felony domestic violence, but under a plea agreement was placed on formal probation, which is still active. He also attends court-ordered domestic violence classes.

Daniel Kavanaugh denies any involvement in the McStay case and has not been named as a suspect.

A few months before they disappeared, Summer filed a child abuse complaint with Child Protective Services against Joseph's oldest son Jonah and his stepfather, Michael McFadden. When the complaint was brought forward, Joseph and Summer were reportedly threatened by McFadden.

McFadden has a criminal history. In 1998, he was charged in the brutal beating of a girlfriend in Orange County, California. The eight-felony-charge included attempted murder; burglary; and assault by means of force, with intent to do great bodily harm. In 2000, McFadden also pleaded guilty to two additional felonies that included terrorist threats and assault, for which he served 15 months in prison.

The CPS investigation was dropped after the family disappeared. With no other living heirs, Jonah would be first in line to inherit the McStay's estate.

McFadden has not been named as a suspect in the McStay disappearance or murder. He denies any involvement.

When the bodies of the McStay family were found in November 2013, the case and all associated agency files were transferred to the San Bernardino County Sheriff's Department's Homicide Detail, where it remains unsolved, but active. San Diego and FBI staff will continue to assist on the case as needed.

The exact method of homicide for each of the McStay's is unknown and the autopsy files are sealed. Authorities would say only that the bodies had been buried for an extended period of time and that there was other evidence at the scene that would be useful to the investigation.

Joseph's father, who has been a vocal critic of the earlier years of the investigation, believes the family was murdered by cold-blooded contract killers, or by individuals who knew that the family – including the children – would be able identify them.

The mystery of the McStay family disappearance and murder has been featured on *America's Most Wanted, Disappeared,* and *Nancy Grace.*

Pearl Eaton

They were known as the Broadway Eatons. In the first two decades of the twentieth century, six of the seven talented Eaton children from Virginia became highly respected stage performers. Three of the girls, Mary, Pearl, and Doris were among the elite – they were also Ziegfeld Girls.

By the 1930s, the golden days of Broadway were gone, the precocious juvenile actors were grown, and the sudden rise and fall from stardom had taken most of the Eaton family down a dismal path. Of the seven, all but one faded into obscurity. Pearl, the one with the most spunk and energy, died alone in a squalid apartment in Southern California. She was murdered. To this day, no one knows why or who committed the crime.

Charles H.S. Eaton, a newspaper printer, and his wife Mary F. Eaton had seven children. The family was native to Virginia and the children were raised in the Portsmouth and Norfolk areas. While all of the children were talented, five of them – Charles, Doris, Joseph, Mary, and Pearl – were performers. Robert, the oldest son, avoided show business and, after a few years in the Army, owned a successful business. The oldest daughter, Evelyn, had no interest in being a stage performer, but dedicated her life to managing the talented family and had three children of her own that were Broadway stars in the 1920s and early 1930s.

In 1911, Pearl, Mary, and Doris were placed under contract to perform at the Shubert Belasco Theatre in Washington, D.C. in a production of *The Blue Bird*. From that point on, the children, and the Eaton family in general, became widely known for their talent and professionalism and, as young performers, worked regularly across the country.

The Ziegfeld Follies was a theatrical production that premiered in 1907. The hugely popular performances were the brainchild of Broadway producer Florenz Ziegfeld, who was simply looking for something to fill New York's summer entertainment calendar. When the Follies became a hit, Ziegfeld started producing the shows each year through 1927, then periodically through 1931. Between 1932, when Ziegfeld died, and 1957, the shows were produced by a variety of people, but never achieved the success of the earlier years.

The Ziegfeld Follies completely changed Broadway. Typical dramatic performances became interspersed with lavish musicals complete with elaborately costumed dancers, spectacular sets, and chorus-line singers. Ziegfeld performers often became movie stars and careers were made by the Follies. Without the genius of Florenz Ziegfeld, the type of Broadway musical that is still enjoyed today would not have been possible.

Between 1918 and 1927, one or more of the Eaton children performed in the Ziegfeld Follies. Mary Eaton held starring roles in three separate editions between 1920 and 1927 and later in two of Ziegfeld's big screen productions. Although never a principal dancer, Pearl Eaton stayed with the Follies the longest, performing in six different editions between 1918 and 1923. Doris Eaton was the longest surviving of the Ziegfeld Girls, dying in September 2010 at the age of 106.

After their initial success in *The Blue Bird*, Pearl, Mary, Doris, and their brother Charles performed together or separately in a large number of plays. Most of their work was as members

of Sylvester Poli's stock theater company (the Poli Players), which had theaters located across the northeast United States.

In 1916, Pearl was appearing in a minor role in a performance of *The Passing Snow*. When the producer decided to take the show on the road, Pearl stayed with the cast. While traveling, she fell in love with one of the show's violinists – Harry Levant. The couple was married in 1917 and the following year had a daughter, who they named after Pearl's sister Doris; they called her Dossie.

Shortly after Dossie's birth, Pearl returned to her career and was soon back at the Winter Garden as a dancer in *Sinbad*. By 1918, she had begun her career with the Ziegfeld Follies, which lasted until 1923. Also in 1923, Pearl again performed with the Poli Stock Company in a starring role at the Majestic Theater in New York City. Afterwards she joined Broadway producer Charles Dillingham's troupe as both a performer and choreographer. Dillingham cast Pearl in the musical comedy *The Love Letter*, and was so impressed with her administrative skills that he hired her as the first female stage manager.

Pearl's sister Doris believed that the Prohibition years (1920-1933) had a marked effect on Pearl's life. In a family biography, she described her as a party girl that loved to dance and, when Prohibition was enacted, Pearl started dancing in many of the illicit New York City speakeasies. Many of the legitimate nightclubs and cabarets had gone out of business and illicit nightclubs became popular gathering places where people could dance and drink all night.

Leaving Dossie with family members, Pearl would finish her evening theater performance and start work around midnight in one of the many underground nightclubs. Performing in floorshows of well-known places like El Fey and Texas Guinan's 300 Club, Pearl not only made extra money, but also met many of New York's finest residents. At the opening of one club, the guest list was described as a Blue Book of New York society – sports figures, entertainers, politicians, and Mob bosses. At El Fey, Pearl was the featured dancer, backed by a chorus of 10, some of whom also had been Ziegfeld girls. One sister described Pearl as made for the 1920s and 1930s and that she had never seemed happier than during that time in her life. She was popular with the nightclub owners and customers and she was well rewarded for her performances. Another sister recalled that Pearl was definitely the rebel in the family, smoking, drinking, and mixing with a fast group that made the Prohibition-era nightclubs and speakeasies their home.

In 1928, Pearl performed in her final show at the Globe Theatre on Broadway. That same year she was honored with a caricature at the famous Sardi's restaurant and was selected by Erno Bakos, a Hungarian portrait artist, to represent the typical American blond. In his quest to find the ideal woman, Bakos felt Pearl Eaton's image was the epitome of American beauty, intelligence, and charm.

Shortly after her final performance in New York, Pearl moved to Los Angeles to work as a choreographer and dance director for RKO studios. Along with the rest of her talented family, Pearl's stage career stalled in the late 1920s and, despite her talent and reputation, she was released from RKO in 1930. By the early 1930s, the face of the entertainment industry was in transition. The days of big stage productions were fading and being replaced with movies staring the likes of Fred Astaire and Ginger Rogers. During this time, Pearl performed in a few small movie roles and briefly opened a small dance studio for children in Encino, California, but her career was essentially over.

In 1931, Pearl married her second husband – Richard Curtis Enderly. Dick Enderly had graduated from the University of California and then the United States Naval Academy at Annapolis. After leaving the military, Enderly became an executive with the Richfield Oil Company and Pearl seemed to be genuinely happy with married life. Then a teenager, Dossie adored her new stepfather.

Unfortunately, the sudden change from Broadway and cabaret entertainer to housewife had a negative effect on Pearl and she, and two of her siblings (Mary and Charles), developed a dependence on both alcohol and prescription drugs. Mary's husband Millard and Pearl's husband Dick were also heavy drinkers and family get-togethers ultimately became little more than drunken brawls. With the exception of Doris, alcohol, drug abuse, and the fall from stardom to mediocrity plagued the Eatons the rest of their lives.

When Richard Enderly died in 1952 of a heart attack, Pearl withdrew from the public and was said rarely to leave her apartment. According to two biographies written some years later – the one by her sister Doris and another by Lauren Redniss – Pearl never overcame her battle with alcohol and drugs and spent most of her days trying to write songs, scripts, and short stories, with no success.

At the age of 60, Pearl Eaton was found dead in her apartment in Manhattan Beach, California, on September 10, 1958. She had been savagely beaten and was lying naked in a pool of blood. According to the homicide report, Pearl's legs and the walls of the apartment were streaked with bloody handprints and the filthy apartment was strewn with magazines.

The cause of death was listed as homicide, but there were never any leads or suspects in the case and the crime was barely mentioned in the news. Pearl Eaton's murder remains unsolved.

Princess Doe

In the early morning hours of July 15, 1982, a maintenance worker found the body of a young girl near the edge of Johnsonburg Creek in Blairstown, New Jersey's, cemetery. Six months later, the girl was buried just a few feet from where she was found. No one knew her name or how she came to be in their town, but about 50 residents attended her funeral and the procession included a full police escort. Community donations paid for the entire service, including a headstone with the inscription:

Princess Doe
Missing From Home
Dead Among Strangers
Remembered By All
Born ? - Found July 15, 1982

After 32 years, the murder remains unsolved and the true identify of Princess Doe is still unknown.

When the girl named Princess Doe was found in the Blairstown cemetery, she was partially clothed, barefoot, and without underwear. The Warren County, New Jersey, Medical Examiner estimated that she was between 14 and 18 years of age and had been murdered from one to three weeks prior to being found. She was not believed to have been murdered where she was found, but killed elsewhere and her body left by the small rural cemetery near Highway 94.

Authorities described the victim as Caucasian, about 5-foot 2 inches tall and 100 pounds, with brown, shoulder-length hair. When found, the young girl was wearing a red short-sleeved shirt with yellow, blue, and black piping; a red, white, and blue wrap-around skirt with a wide border of peacocks near the hem; and a necklace with white beads along the chain holding an ornate 14 karat gold cross. After descriptions of the clothing were released to the media, three women contacted authorities stating they had purchased identical items in the Long Island, New York, area.

The fingernails of Princess Doe's right hand were painted with red nail polish and both ears were pierced – the left ear twice. Although the body was partially decomposed, it bore no other distinguishing marks.

Examination of Princess Doe's teeth showed that the two front teeth were slightly darker than the others. The dental examination also showed that she had fillings in four of her molars. Her dental records were widely distributed, but there were no replies.

The child's blood type was determined to be O. Fingerprints were taken and checked against more than 50 million others in the FBI's database, with no match.

Sketch artists made renderings of what they thought the child might have looked like and the Smithsonian Institution later created a three-dimensional composite using a CT scan of her skull. The sketches were, and continue to be, widely disseminated to the media. Based on her dental care, the type of clothing she wore, and the gold crucifix found with the body, Princess Doe is believed to be from a middle class family, yet no one has come forward to identify her.

Princess Doe died from a brutal beating; there was no weapon found near the body. Severe skull fractures were probably caused by a pipe or bat. The beating was so savage that her facial features and eye color could not be determined. Due to the level of decomposition, there were no confirmed signs of sexual assault

In September 1999, Princess Doe's body was exhumed and samples taken from her femur for DNA testing in Baltimore, Maryland. Within 3 hours, the child was reburied in the same grave. Testing of samples from her clothing point to European descent, and DNA analysis of her hair and teeth indicate that she spent time in the Long Island, New York area, just prior to her death. The samples further reveal that she was originally from somewhere in the western United States, most likely Arizona, but that at periods in her life she was transient – possibly a runaway.

DNA testing also showed markers that are not part of Princess Doe's profile. These small traces of DNA may represent the killer, or at least someone who was with her around the time she was murdered. Multiple samples of Princess Doe's DNA are available for comparison in the FBI's Combined DNA Index System (CODIS).

From the first day that Princess Doe was found in the dense woods of Cedar Ridge Cemetery, the crime has haunted the community of Blairstown and law enforcement personnel investigating its details. Lt. Eric Krantz, who was the first police officer at the scene worked the case daily for more than 25 years. It was Krantz who gave the unidentified victim the name Princess Doe, dressed a department store mannequin in the clothes the girl was wearing, and then invited the media to a press conference to generate interest in the case. Even after retiring from the Blairstown police in 1985, Krantz has periodically returned to Blairstown to speak at graveside memorial services.

Detective Stephen Spiers of the Warren County Prosecutor's Office, who has since retired as well, became the lead investigator on the case in 1998 and appeared on a CNN segment about the crime in 2012. Spiers has been instrumental in obtaining DNA testing each time the process is refined. Both Krantz and Spiers actively follow the case.

The only known Blairstown residents to have seen the girl alive were Ann Latimer and her 6-year-old daughter. Both noticed the girl on the morning of July 13 in a shopping center across the street from where her body was found 2 days later. Latimer, a registered nurse, later stated that it was the unusual pattern of peacocks in the young girl's skirt that drew them to her.

Over the decades, there have been various theories about the identity of Princess Doe and her killer. Some have been easily disproved; others remain viable. Among them are:

- Early in the case, Princess Doe was believed to be Diane Dye, a missing child from California. DNA testing conclusively proved that the two girls were not the same.
- Authorities at one time thought Princess Doe was a runaway working as a hotel housekeeper in Ocean City, Maryland, but

there has been insufficient information to prove or disprove the theory.

- Attempts to link Princess Doe with men believed to have committed vicious crimes in the early 1980s have not been substantiated. These included John Reese, who savagely killed a woman in nearby Belvidere, New Jersey, in 1989; serial killer Henry Lee Lucas, who murdered at least 11 people in Michigan, Texas, and Florida between 1960 and 1983; and Joel Rifkan, whose confirmed crime spree is believed to have spanned the years between 1989 and 1993. There is no conclusive link between Princess Doe's murder and any of these men.
- Authorities believe Princess Doe spent time in the Long Island, New York area. This is partially substantiated by the DNA analysis of her hair that showed her living in the northeast United States within 5 months from the time her body was found. The recollection of Ann Latimer and the dress Princess Doe was wearing 2 days before she was found crosschecked with three women who told police they had purchased identical clothing at shops in Long Island.
- One tip to the police indicated that Princess Doe had been a prostitute working at the local truck stop. Police interviewed numerous truckers and service personnel, but no one admitted to seeing or knowing the girl.
- In October 1991, the body of a woman known only as the Tiger Lady was found in nearby Knowlton Township. The body was one of at least five murdered women left along New Jersey's Interstate 80 in 1993. The connection between the Tiger Lady, so called because of the tattoo of a crouching tiger on her left calf, and Princess Doe was largely based on the location where the body was found – Warren County – and the method of death – brutal bludgeoning of the head, essentially eradicating any facial features. Police do not believe the two cases are linked, but a connection has not been completely ruled out.

Perhaps the most promising direction for solving Princess Doe's murder lies with Arthur and Donna Kinlaw, who operated a prostitution ring from Hunt's Point, New York, in the early 1980s. The couple is associated with a string of crimes across the United States that, in addition to prostitution, included welfare and bank fraud, burglary, and murder. Donna alone was arrested more than 50 times, had 17 aliases, and used at least seven different Social Security numbers.

In 1998, the Kinlaws were arrested in California for falsely using the name of one of their Hunt's Point prostitutes in a welfare scam. When authorities located the prostitute, she voluntarily provided information that implicated the couple in a series of at least four murders committed by Arthur and witnessed by his wife, Donna. Each woman was murdered because they refused to be a part of Arthur's prostitution ring.

Kinlaw murdered his victims in a variety of ways – strangulation, stabbing, shooting, and bludgeoning. In the latter, he typically used an aluminum baseball bat. In those cases, the victims were savagely struck in the head and dumped at a different location. Given similarities between known Kinlaw crimes and that of Princess Doe, authorities questioned the couple about their possible involvement. Arthur admitted to the murder of Princess Doe and implicated Donna as having been in the Blairstown cemetery when she was killed. Neither could, or would, provide the true name of the girl they had killed, but Donna recalled that she was from Long Island and was able to provide a description that matched existing forensics sketches.

For the known crimes, Arthur Kinlaw was convicted on two counts of second-degree murder and is currently serving a 20-year sentence at the Sullivan Correctional Facility in Fallsburg New York; he is eligible for parole in 2018. Donna pleaded guilty to manslaughter and was given a reduced sentence for testifying against Arthur; she was released from prison in October 2003 from the Albion Correctional Facility in Albion, New York.

A link between the Kinlaws and Princess Doe has not been confirmed, largely because the girl remains unidentified. Until her true name, whereabouts, and family connections are verified, associating Princess Doe with the Kinlaws and their nefarious activities in the New York and New Jersey areas cannot be proven. Despite their confessions, they have not been charged with the crime.

The case of Princess Doe has received nationwide media exposure. In April 1983, just a few months after she was buried, Home Box Office produced a television special about Princess Doe that featured details of the crime, the investigation, and her funeral. The 20-minute video is still available on YouTube. The same year (1983), FBI Director William Webster announced the establishment of a database for missing persons and unsolved crimes. Known as the National Crime Information Center (NCIC), the computerized index provides criminal justice agencies with details about a variety of crimes. Princess Doe was the first case entered into the new system. Over the decades since the discovery of her body, she has become a symbol of missing person's cases.

The unsolved crime and missing person's case of Princess Doe was featured in a CNN television network segment on September 24, 2012. The segment, which featured an interview with Detective Spiers, presented updated information on the case and displayed the newly completed recreation of her face produced by the Smithsonian. *America's Most Wanted* also featured the Princess Doe case in late September 2012. Current efforts include having the episode re-aired.

There have been two novels based on this crime. The first – *Death Among Strangers* – was published in 1998 by Diedre Laikens. The second – *The Untold Story of Princess Doe* – was published in 2012 by a former Blairstown resident, Christie Napurano. Although they are fiction, each contains accurate information about the crime and descriptions of the community and both are partially responsible for keeping the public's interest in the case active.

A website dedicated to the Princess Doe crime (princessdoe.org) is periodically updated and maintained by a former Blairstown resident, and four issues of *Weird New Jersey* (Issues 10, 13, 14, and 29) have included articles about the unsolved crime. Princess Doe is also listed in the National Missing and Unidentified (NamUS) database, the National Center for Missing and Exploited Children, and Porchlight for the Missing. The New Jersey State Police maintains a page about the crime (njsp.org) as well.

Periodically memorial services for Princess Doe are held in the Cedar Ridge Cemetery. In 2012, on the 30th anniversary of her discovery, more than 100 attended. A high level of emotional attachment to the case remains in the Blairstown area and the community continues to support efforts to identify the young girl and apprehend her killer.

As of March 2014, the Warren County Prosecutor's Office Cold Case Unit is in charge of the case. It remains open and active.

Walker Family Murders

The Clifford Walker family lived on the Palmer Ranch, in Osprey, Florida. Their small white frame ranch house was secluded, but well situated for Cliff to tend the Palmer's cattle. The property also was popular with hunters, and there was a good fishing stream nearby.

The Walker's led a simple but good life and, on the weekend before Christmas 1959, the family shopped in Sarasota, visited with friends, and then headed home around 4 P.M. for dinner. When fellow ranch hand and friend Don McLeod arrived early the following morning to take Cliff hunting, the entire Walker family of four lay dead in the house.

In the morning of December 19, 1959, the Clifford Walker family drove 12 miles north from rural Osprey, Florida, to Sarasota to Christmas shop. With a new child, the family of four needed a bigger car, so part of their day was spent browsing at Altman Chevrolet. Although the family test-drove a Hudson Jet, witnesses at the dealership later recalled that they were also browsing a two-tone, 1956 Chevrolet Bel Air. That morning, the family also stopped for groceries at the IGA and, later, visited Johnny's Hardware to pick up penny candy for the children and a carton of Kool cigarettes for Cliff.

Promising to visit their friends in the afternoon, the Walker's stopped at the home of Don and Lucy McLeod on the way home from Sarasota. In exchange for ranching chores, Cliff, Don, and their families lived in small ranch houses on the 100,000-acre Palmer Ranch; their homes were about 20 minutes apart. While the wives and children visited, the men went to nearby Cow Pen Slough on a short hunting trip. After returning, the two friends loaded a jeep with cattle feed for Cliff to take home and arranged to meet early the following morning to hunt wild hogs.

At about 3:45 P.M. Christine (age 24) left the McLeod's house in the family car. Cliff (age 25) and the two children – Jimmie (age 3) and Debbie (23 months) – left for home in the jeep about 4 P.M.

Police timelines indicate that Christine arrived home at about 4:05 P.M., but did not park the car in her normal spot, likely because someone was already parked there. Christine entered the home, hung her purse in the kitchen, placed Lucy McLeod's Christmas card on top of the refrigerator, and put the day's purchases away. Given the short time associated with the subsequent events and Cliff's arrival about 15 minutes after Christine, the unknown person would have watched Christine complete those chores from either inside or outside the house.

There are varying theories about exactly what precipitated it, but the events of the crime are not in dispute. The unidentified person (or persons) first hit Christine in the face on the Walker's porch, bruising her left cheek. Fighting back, Christine hit the assailant with her high-heel shoe drawing blood. No doubt angered, the man beat her severely, raped her on Jimmie's bed, and then shot her in the head twice with a .22-caliber weapon. The first shot grazed her hairline; the second shot was through the top of her head and killed her instantly. The killer then took quilts from Jimmie's bed, wiped blood from Christine's body, and dragged her to the living room floor.

Having stopped to put air in the jeep's tires, Cliff and the children arrived home about 4:35 P.M. Unaware of what had just transpired, Cliff had no reason to take the loaded rifle in the jeep with him. When he opened the door, he was immediately shot through the right eye and died instantly.

Three-year-old Jimmie still holding a lollipop from Johnny's Hardware was murdered next. The killer placed the gun inches from the boy's face and fired once, but the child did not die quickly enough and the assailant fired twice more into his upper forehead. The child was later found curled up next to his father.

At only 23 months, Debbie tried to crawl to her mother. Bloodstains showed that she was shot next to her mother's body, but did not die. Perhaps out of bullets, the killer carried the little girl to the bathroom, stuffed a sock in the broken bathtub drain to fill the tub, and held her under the water until she was dead.

When the carnage was over, the killer locked the doors, and simply walked away.

At 5:30 A.M. on December 20, 1959, Don McLeod arrived at the Walker home to pick up Cliff for their morning hunt. As later described to the police, McLeod expected to see signs that Walker was up and making coffee, but instead he found the house quiet and dark. An undecorated Christmas tree and four wrapped gifts addressed to the children were on the front porch.

McLeod saw nothing unusual through the windows and all the doors were locked, so he used his pocketknife to cut the back screen door and unlatch the hook. Finding the interior door unlocked, McLeod entered the kitchen, switched on a light, and discovered a gruesome crime scene that included the bodies of his four friends.

Afraid the killer was still in the house, McLeod ran outside and jumped in the jeep to go for help. The cattle feed and loaded rifle were where he had seen them the afternoon before. McLeod's first stop was the nearby IGA market, but having no money for the payphone, he continued on to a restaurant. The owner, who was just opening for the day, had no telephone, but gave McLeod a dime to call the Sarasota police, who relayed the message to the Sarasota County Sheriff's Office. Badly shaken, all McLeod could say was *they're all dead!*

The first officer at the scene was 20-year-old Sheriff Ross Boyer. As Boyer later recounted, the home was a *clue-laden mess*. Overwhelmed at what they saw and inexperienced at such a horrific crime, the investigators inadvertently contaminated the scene when gathering evidence – not the least of which was their reliance on a newspaper photographer and reporter to document the crime scene. One deputy also tracked through pools of blood leaving prints from his cowboy boot that left investigators thinking they belonged to the killer. Despite those unfortunate mistakes, authorities collected a lot of evidence that appeared in the photographs and, many years later, were tested for DNA. Among the evidence collected were:

- Christine's high-heel shoe full of blood from the killer
- A cigarette wrapper from a brand that Cliff did not smoke
- Fingerprints (or a palm print) on the bathtub faucet handle where Debbie was drowned
- Seven spent .22-caliber bullet shells. The murder weapon was not recovered and whether it was a rifle or a handgun has never been determined. The spent shells, however, had unique firing pin marks that would make them easily identifiable if the murder weapon was found.
- Hair samples (one blond and one black)
- A white T-shirt with grease
- Semen on Christine's clothes.

Family members noted several items missing from the Walker home. Among these were the Walker's marriage certificate that was seen on the living room wall the day before the murder; Christine's majorette uniform from high school; a carton of Kool cigarettes that the Walkers bought the day before the crime while shopping in Sarasota; and Cliff's pocketknife with a fruit tree design on the handle.

A couple of months after the murder, bloody clothes were found in a shed about a mile from the Walker home. The clothes belonged to Cliff and Christine, and included two men's shirts, a skirt, a blouse, pants, and a handkerchief. With DNA not yet an available crime scene technique, Sheriff Boyer believed the items had been used by the killer to clean blood from himself. Police questioned fishermen who might have been in the area the night of the crime, but no one reported seeing anyone at, or near the shed.

Over the decades there have been several theories and hundreds of suspects interviewed about the Walker murders. Most of the suspects have been cleared through questioning and confirmed alibis and, in later years, through DNA analysis. Although Sarasota County sheriffs and deputies have changed over the years, most of them have clung to the theory that whoever killed the Walkers knew them. A stranger would not have gotten by the family's hounds and there would have been no logical reason for a stranger to kill children too young to make an identification.

In the early months and years of the investigation, the suspects included a cousin (Elbert Walker), an electric company meter reader (Stanley Mauck), and a 65-year-old railroad worker (Wilbur Tooker). All of the early suspects were familiar with the ranch and would have known about the shed where the bloody clothes were found.

The cousin – Elbert Walker – was described by friends and family as a heavy drinker and often confrontational. His behavior after the deaths seemed inappropriate to some and he had information about the crime that had not been released to the media. Over the decades, Elbert Walker was questioned several times, but he passed multiple polygraph tests, and the consensus was that he was not the killer. In 2004, DNA testing proved he was not a match.

The Walkers were on the meter reader's route and he reportedly had some psychiatric issues that included the urge to kill his wife and children. Mauck's wife later told police that her husband was devastated by the Walker murders and eventually had a nervous breakdown. Stanley Mauck died in 1997.

Wilbur Tooker lived about a mile from the Walker home and often visited the family. Christine repeatedly told family and friends that she was afraid of Tooker and that he had made many unwanted advances towards her. Tooker's alibi was not firm for the night of the murders, but he was never arrested or charged with the crime. Tooker died in 1963 and it is unclear whether his DNA profile has been tested against the crime scene evidence. As a result, Tooker remains a viable suspect.

The suspects most often discussed in the press included a friend, an ex-high school boyfriend, and an infamous pair of murders who were later the subject of headline news and a best selling book and movie – *In Cold Blood*.

Don McLeod was the obvious suspect from the very beginning. He found the bodies, was very familiar with the family and ranch, and some thought his interest in Christine was more than neighborly. McLeod remained a suspect for years, even after passing multiple polygraph tests, and many Osprey locals went to their graves convinced he was the killer. In 2004, Don McLeod was officially excluded after DNA testing proved he did not match the semen on Christine's clothing.

Curtis McCall was reportedly Christine's high school sweetheart, although he told authorities in the early 1960s that they had never dated. After the murder, McCall family members told police they were convinced that Christine and McCall were having an affair. McCall's cousin also told police he had become unstable, very nervous, and had lost a lot of weight following the crime.

Police described McCall as a troublemaker. He had a history of violence and was fired from his dispatcher's job with the Florida Highway Patrol. McCall at one time owned a nine-shot .22-caliber pistol, but told authorities that he sold it and didn't remember to whom.

After questioning on numerous occasions, McCall undertook three polygraph tests. On each occasion, the technician felt McCall was nervous and seemed to be withholding information about the Walker murders.

McCall left the Sarasota area after taking the polygraphs and has not been seen or questioned since. His whereabouts are currently unknown, so his guilt or innocence is still in question.

In 1994, a Stroudsburg, Florida, bartender contacted the Sarasota County Sheriff's Department stating that a regular customer had confessed to killing some people in Osprey when he was younger and mentioned the name Walker. The man was described as a white male in his 60s and a gun enthusiast. Neither the suspect nor the bartender was ever located, but authorities theorized that the man might be McCall.

Richard Eugene Hickock and Perry Edward Smith were the subject of Truman Capote's *In Cold Blood*. On the night of November 15, 1959, just one month before the Walker family was killed, the pair murdered the Herbert Clutter family on a rural wheat farm near Holcomb, Kansas. The motive was $10,000 that Hickock and Smith thought the family had in a home safe. When they discovered that was not true, they killed the Clutters to leave no witnesses.

After the crime, the two killers stole a few items from the Clutter house, fled Kansas, and drove around the country in a two-tone Chevrolet for about 45 days. Witnesses placed Hickock and Smith in the Osprey area between December 17 and 19, the day the Walker's were killed, and authorities have theorized that the pair saw the Walkers when they were browsing cars in Sarasota and later used the vehicle as a ruse.

Hickock and Smith were eventually arrested in Las Vegas, Nevada, on December 31, 1959, convicted of first-degree murder, sentenced to death, and executed by hanging on April 14, 1965.

Although there are similarities in the two crimes, authorities in Florida have not been able to definitively link Hickock and Smith to the Walker murders. The similarities and differences include:

1. The crimes were committed one month apart, but 1,600 miles from each other.
2. Each crime involved the murder of a family of four living in a rural farmhouse.
3. All four members of each family were shot in the face and/or head. The clutters were bound, the Walkers were not.
4. There were semen stains on the bodies of the two wives – Bonnie Clutter and Christine Walker.

5. The motive for the Walker crime remains unclear, but the family was not wealthy and the only items stolen were of sentimental value. The motive for the Clutter murders was financial.
6. A blonde hair and a dark hair were found at both homes, but there were no skin cells to match DNA
7. Fingerprints on the Walker's bathtub faucet did not match either Hickock or Smith, although the print was believed to be a palm print, yet checked against fingerprints.
8. Hickock and Smith would not have known about the shed where the bloody clothes were found.
9. The Clutters were killed with a 12-guage shotgun; the Walkers were killed with a .22-caliber weapon.
10. Neither Hickock nor Smith ever confessed to the Walker murder; both took polygraph tests and passed.
11. While witnesses claimed to have seen the two men near Osprey at the time of the crime, they were only recognized after authorities circulated photographs of them.
12. In December 2012, the bodies of Hickock and Smith were exhumed from their graves at the Lansing Correctional Facility cemetery and DNA samples taken from their leg bones. The DNA analysis proved inconclusive. According to authorities, the samples were too degraded to match the profiles and there was potential contamination from many years of handling and storage.

As of March 2014, there are no plans to request further DNA analysis of any of the suspects or crime scene evidence, but the case remains open. The murder of the Walker family is the oldest unsolved crime in the history of the Sarasota County Sheriff's Department.

Printed in Great Britain
by Amazon